Breaking Free From Wedlock Deadlock

Overcoming Destructive Myths By Embracing Christian Truths

Paul A. Mickey

Epworth Church Library
3002 Hope Valley Rd.
Durham, NC 27707

BREAKING FREE FROM WEDLOCK DEADLOCK
Overcoming Destructive Myths By Embracing Christian Truths
Copyright © 1989 by Paul A. Mickey
Published by Bristol Books

First Edition, February 1989

All rights reserved. Except for brief quotations embodied in critical articles and reviews, no part of this book may be used or reproduced in any manner without written permission.

All Scripture is taken from *The Holy Bible, New International Version*. Copyright ©1973, 1978, 1984 International Bible Society. Used by permission.

Library of Congress Card Number: 88-72131
ISBN: 0-917851-16-1
Suggested Subject Category:
1. Marriage
Recommended Dewey Decimal Classification: 248.4

BRISTOL BOOKS
An imprint of Good News, A Forum for Scriptural Christianity, Inc.
308 East Main Street • Wilmore, Kentucky, 40390

Contents

Acknowledgments	7
Introduction	9
1. But I've Never Committed Adultery	19
2. But I've Held the Marriage Together	39
3. I Don't Get Sex	57
4. Do You Like It? Charge It!	75
5. I'm Getting an Attorney	93
6. We've Simply Grown Apart	113
7. I'll Hang on 'til the Children Are Grown	135
8. You Have to Peel Your Own Shrimp	153

To Martin and Granvillene Carter,
fellow pilgrims in marriage and life

Acknowledgments

The lives of many individuals and couples are part of this study. And those that read, I trust, will be further helped in the knowledge that they are assisting others to obtain freedom from the bondage of a wedlock deadlock and to build a marriage that makes life worth living together.

James Robb and the staff at Bristol Books have shown the third and fourth mile of *agape* love toward me in this project. I'm glad that we are family in Christ and that they love me the way they do.

Ginny Ashmore made the project happen. Without her unbelievable energy, wise critiques and supple knowledge of how computers and people work, literally all would have been lost. Her support and cheerfulness through the project make it all worthwhile.

My wife, Jane, and our children, Sandi and Bruce, smile all too knowingly when I'm in the midst of a writing project: "Watch out! He'll soon be through." And so I am, and I deeply love them for their support and generosity of spirit, energy, humor and critique of me and my work.

Finally, I want to acknowledge Duke University that afforded me a sabbatical in Spring 1988 that allowed me to complete this manuscript. I trust this work will bring honor to the University.

Introduction

Recently the senior pastor of a large, suburban Southern Baptist church called me about a marriage break-up in his congregation. For years the Southern Baptist Convention has taken pride in its stand against divorce. This minister was concerned because divorce, marital conflict and remarriage of divorced individuals has been nearly as common in his congregation as in more liberal churches.

"We have it everywhere," he worried. "What do we do to keep the Christian marriage from falling apart?" His was a legitimate pastoral concern and a powerful theological question. At the heart of his question was a frightful, accurate perception: Christians, including those in conservative evangelical congregations, have a high divorce rate that rivals society in general. Why are Christians divorcing at such a rapid rate? Why have we lost our distinctiveness as Christians? What must we do to correct it? Why have we not *really* heard what has been preached and taught about the Christian family?

This pastor's question is echoed by many. Other lay people and pastors simply turn their heads. They avoid the reminders of the number of divorces in their congregations. In such situations a couple often disappears from the church when a break-up occurs. Or, one partner leaves the fellowship. The congregation concludes that the remaining spouse is the innocent victim. Instead, the one remaining may have driven away the more faithful partner.

The fact remains that divorce is everywhere—outside *and* inside the church. As Christians we must acknowledge that divorce exists and adopt realistic ways to help people cope with their marital conflicts. Otherwise they will divide Christ's community of faith. We must learn how to overcome and redeem the "wedlock deadlock" syndrome in the church family.

Divorce is another manifestation of original sin. Being born again, being saved, being Spirit-filled and joining a congregation that teaches and preaches against divorce, adultery and fornication does not negate the wiles of the serpent. Temptations exist; humans are fallible. Christians do not have a magic pill to immunize themselves against divorce. The starting point for conquering this problem must be the admission that we "all have sinned and fall short of the glory of God" (Romans 3:23).

My purpose in this book is to examine eight popular myths Christians use to rationalize divorce. I want to dispel those myths through the truth of the gospel. I believe that the average Christian has access to the proper teaching, understanding and adequate philosophical and psychological foundation for living an effective, joyous and satisfying marriage relationship. But it takes the correct orientation and commitment, plus hard work! Marriage can be the most rewarding and satisfying of human experiences and, by the same token, it can be the most frustrating and agonizing. Marriages may be joined in heaven, but they are lived on earth. In my book *Tough Marriage* I endeavor to address the twelve most difficult and rewarding aspects of a marriage. If these "twelve commandments" are followed, I believe a marriage can be a strong, resilient and rewarding experience. God's intention is for marriage to succeed. But the popular myths that put marriages in jeopardy of "wedlock deadlock" must be overcome by Christian truths.

In order to separate myth from reality, let's look at some foundational truths that evangelicals have distorted.

The Man Is the Spiritual Head of a House

Christian husbands and wives often deadlock over the teaching of St. Paul in Ephesians 5 that the Christian relationship is one of mutual servanthood, humility and sacrificial leadership.

Sometimes men demand absolute authority over their wives, expect them to keep the house in perfect condition while working full time and want them to be alluring lovers as well. They think this is leadership. But in this scenario the wife is reduced to a household servant and source of inexpensive sexual gratification. This interpretation of leadership is not consistent with Scripture.

On the other hand, some women have unreasonably high expections of their husbands based on their ideal of what a husband should be like as spiritual head of the household. Frustrated, these women complain about their husbands' inadequacies instead of respecting them.

To be the spiritual head of a household requires more mutuality than most cases of wedlock deadlock reveal. The wife is to be submissive to the husband because she *chooses* to be submissive in the same way the believer chooses to be submissive to the yoke of obedience to Christ. By the same token, the husband is the spiritual head of a household, not by status or by gender, but because he sacrificially gives himself for wife and home in the same way that Christ gave himself for the Church. Many Christian men rebel against popular myths that the wife is submissive only to a husband who leads in the way she dictates. Being the spiritual head of a household is not a unilateral or an authoritarian role. To arbitrarily push a husband into an "activist," spiritual, head-of-household role creates marital and spiritual havoc.

A Woman's Place Is in the Home

Many men and women believe a woman's proper role in the home is to be a Martha. In the story of Jesus' relationship with Mary, Martha and Lazarus (Luke 10:38-42) it is clear all three were Jesus' close personal friends, and he loved them. Martha found her affirmation in preparing meals. Jesus loved good meals and mealtime fellowship, and he never faulted Martha for her choice of a kitchen ministry. But Jesus confronted Martha when she criticized Mary for not staying in the kitchen with her.

Yes, I'll Feed the Sheep but—

Sometimes a husband or wife refuses to take responsibility for meeting his or her share of the family's needs. There may be good intentions as he says, "Yes, I'll do it," but his actions say, "No, I won't do it." The idea is simply to get the nagging partner to back down.

This problem reminds me of the seaside breakfast conversation between Peter and Jesus (John 21:15-19) where the Lord told Peter to feed the sheep. Jesus wants Peter to move beyond a "Yes, but—" formula. He made certain that Peter was challenged three times to feed the sheep. Jesus wanted to make sure that Peter would follow through with his commitment, and church history confirms that this commitment was honored. In the same way, today the sheep of a Christian marriage need to be fed. Partners need to change their "Yes, but—" to "Yes," and get on with the task of nurturing the family.

As Long as We Both Shall Love

This paraphrase of the wedding vows has become a classic distortion of traditional Christian marriage commitment. The traditional language of the marriage ceremony is "until death us do part." A younger generation has decided to write its own marriage vows. Phrases like "as long as we both shall love" keep popping up. Such popular myths of marital commitment are a sure prescription for deadlock and eventual disaster.

The commitment is "for better or for worse, in sickness and in health, in wealth or in poverty." In short, the commitment must remain a commitment, even when the partners don't *feel* like loving.

Rediscovering Christian Truths

Now that we have described some poor attitudes that damage marriages, we will discuss truths which, properly applied, will assist in making Christian marriages stronger.

God Is Head of the Household of Faith

Neither husband nor wife is the real spiritual head of the

house. That is reserved for God as revealed in Jesus Christ. This truth calls both husband and wife to develop a spirit of humility and mutual submission to each other. As human beings we are called upon to submit ourselves to God as head of our households.

We affirm Christ as head of our lives and our homes because of his humility, not arrogance (Philippians 2:5-11). He doesn't dictate how the household must be run. He invites; he humbles himself; he is obedient, he is compassionate.

Wives cannot force husbands to become spiritual heads of the households anymore than the Jewish people could force God to send a Messiah on their terms. The world had to accept Jesus' coming in power and majesty as an infant child. Husbands gain their authority and power as heads of households not because wives and children demand it or because God gives them spiritually aggressive personalities. In Christ they find the power to provide the leadership and guidance sufficient for their families. Even when the doubts of marital deadlock assail, we are encouraged by the words of St. Paul in 2 Corinthians 12:9, "My grace is sufficient for you, for my power is made perfect in weakness."

As Christians We are Called to Live in a Covenant Relationship with God

In Christ, we are invited as individuals and as marriage partners to join in a covenant relationship. No one can be forced to be a good servant. We can't force someone to be humble, obedient or compassionate. The difficult aspect of a covenant relationship is that the initiator, the husband, exercises power and leadership. Through his humility, obedience, commitment and compassion, he invites family members to join in making the family and the marriage work.

This covenant relationship is for mutual edification, upbuilding and growth in life and faith. Our ultimate call for obedience is to Christ and not to obey or demand obedience simply because we happen to be male or female.

The commitment in a marriage is to develop the relationship

and mutual support. The key teaching of Philippians 2 is that Jesus became head of the Church because he chose to offer himself for the sake of others. In response, we become eternally grateful for the salvation offered in Christ. In the marriage relationship, a wife exalts her husband because of his humility, obedience and commitment.

There Is neither Male nor Female

When St. Paul uses these words (Galatians 3:28) he does not at all imply that men and women cease to exist within the kingdom, that there is no sexuality or that sexual differences do not exist. The claim is for a faith relationship and a marriage relationship that affirms our equality in Christ: no one is morally or spiritually superior to another. Differences of sexuality, socio-economic status, race and other biological, social, economic and educational differences begin to fall into their respective order. If this truth of equality can be asserted, then both obvious and subtle differences find their proper places in the marriage relationship.

Husband/Wife Is an I/Thou Relationship

Frequently Christian husbands boast, "My woman is going to obey me." This is wrong because it betrays the very spirit and purpose of the incarnation of Jesus. Because Christ humbled himself for the believer and the church, the strength of a marriage relationship is in the I/Thou relationship of husband and wife. A truly I/Thou encounter acknowledges the truth and reality of the other and shows the belief that each has something to contribute to the other. We can't force obedience or trust. We invite as we move toward a truly I/Thou encounter in marriage.

I consider the three M's of the I/Thou relationship of husband and wife theologically essential for rediscovering Christian truths about the marriage. The successful marriage requires (1) *mutual* invitation, (2) *mutual* choice and (3) *mutual* encounter. Both husband and wife need to invite each other into their lives as spiritual, emotional and personal helpmates. The mutual invitation of I/Thou means no part of life is hidden or potentially unavailable for the building of mutual trust. In the second "M" husband and wife make a self-conscious mutual choice to commit to one another, to be subservient to one another, to honor one another, to work together on the marriage. Unless there is mutual choice by husband and wife, the I/Thou relationship is destroyed and the covenant will be broken. The third element, mutual encounter, is the most difficult. This calls for mutual vulnerability, mutual concern and care for one another at the deepest levels of human existence.

Feeding Your Sheep

The I/Thou relationship, the mutual encounters of husband and wife, and the honoring of one another will foster good marriage relationships. When Jesus' challenged Peter to feed his sheep, he encouraged him to go beyond his "Yes, but—" syndrome. Peter had to break out of the old pattern that had led to betrayal, denial, guilt and self-rejection. In the same way that Jesus asked Peter to feed his sheep, Jesus fed Peter at their seashore breakfast. It was not feeding the multitudes. It was the intimate setting of Jesus caring for his lost sheep—in this case Peter—and inviting that redeemed lamb to care for other sheep.

Consistency in honoring the relationship is essential for a successful marriage. The sheep of the family need to be fed day after day after day. The consistency of commitment to feed the sheep makes the marriage relationship stronger.

Until Death Do Us Part

No marriage will long succeed if its foundation is built solely on the sands of emotion. In the early stages of courtship and marriage, emotions run high and positive. Eventually the couple will come to discover some pain in the growth of their marriage relationship. Developing an I/Thou encounter, fulfilling a covenant relationship and engaging in the three M's of marriage require a tremendous amount of work and no small amount of pain. But a deeper satisfaction will follow if a couple will commit to a more substantial relationship than merely an emotional one.

Many Christians who have gone through a previous marriage or marriages and are in their second or third marriages openly admit what is obvious to me. Had they worked as hard on their first marriages as they are compelled to on the subsequent ones, the first ones would have worked. They are confessing a basic Christian truth: if a marriage is going to work, it must be a commitment "till death us do part." Marriage, like faith, comes out of love, mutuality and trust, but it requires relentless work to succeed. There is no easy formula, no shortcut. And certainly the idea that the emotion of love will hold the marriage together needs correcting. The commitment must not last only until the emotions get tired.

He Who Takes the Plow of the Kingdom Dares Not Look Back

The radical nature of the Christian faith is the call both to the present and the future. We all sin and fall short of the glory of God. We all have ideas, models, fears and previous experiences (both bad and good) that continuously invite us to look back over our shoulders, instead of straight ahead. The call of the Christian life and the Christian marriage is to be centered in Jesus and in the future. The new models, the new relationships, the new directions for our lives are found by pressing ahead and not being consumed by the past. Indeed, we are asked to walk by faith. We must learn to trust God to take care of what's been done as well as to lead us in the right direction in the future. But, having taken hold of the plow of faith or of Christian marriage, we are committed to the future.

We Must Come Under Authority

Christian marriage is a sacred institution because it is ordained by Christ under the authority and power of the church. When a couple asks a church to bless the marriage by holding the service in a church and having clergy officiate, they are making a statement, offering a witness and acknowledging the seriousness of the institution of marriage. They are no longer free as individuals; they are under authority. They are in a covenant relationship. The head of their household is Christ.

As far as the Christian is concerned there is no "free standing" marriage. There is no "open marriage." All marriages are accountable not only to the marriage partners but also to the community of faith, and finally they are accountable to God through Jesus Christ.

Lifetime Partnership Marriage Is a Means of Grace for Us

We are not saved by marriage. However, for those who marry, married life is a Christian vocation. It is a lifetime partnership. It is the most significant and spiritually powerful relationship one can enter into with another human being. The commitment to lifelong marriage is a commitment to being a channel through which God continues to offer grace, love, forgiveness and newness of life.

This book is an effort to detail the essential truths of a Christian marriage in order to dispel the popular myths about marriage and offer corrective teachings about Christian marriage. It is quite clear that the institution of marriage is one of the chief means by which God honors the Church and himself. It is also painfully apparent that the marriages of many believers are in serious trouble. The purpose of this book is not simply to fix troubled marriages. Its larger purpose is to correct false teaching about Christian marriage and to provide a more faithful model by which Christians can begin to pattern their lives and their marriages. Then Christ will be truly honored and their marriages will be seen as a source of power, renewing transformation and hope for the future.

One

But I've Never Committed Adultery

Popular Myth:
Sexual Adultery Is the Only Real Sin Against a Marriage

Christian Truth:
But the Fruit of the Spirit is . . .

Popular Myth:
Sexual Adultery Is the Only Real Sin Against a Marriage

Sexual faithfulness is essential in maintaining a good marriage relationship. Moreover, for the Christian, faithfulness is an expectation reinforced by Scripture beginning with the seventh commandment, "You shall not commit adultery." This principle was reinforced and expanded by Jesus when he said, "You have heard that it was said, 'Do not commit adultery.' But I tell you that anyone who looks at a woman lustfully has already committed adultery with her in his heart" (Matthew 5:27-28).

While adultery is forbidden in the evangelical tradition, Christians have embraced a popular myth which says, "If I've never committed adultery in my marriage, I am safe. I've covered my spiritual and marital bases." Surprise! The Christian *truth* that contributes to a healthy and successful marriage is not limited to sexual fidelity. The good Christian marriage is built upon the fruit of the Spirit that produce love, obedience and fidelity of heart, mind and body.

This myth covers up several realities of marriage deadlock. One reality is that assessing blame in an adulterous relationship may not be as simple as it seems. Rarely does the blame for an affair lie solely with one partner. Take the case of Joan* and John.

*All names have been changed.

Joan burst through my office door one day, nearly speechless with anger. "I cannot believe this. My husband of twenty-five years is having an affair. And he is a Christian! How could he do this to me?"

Joan, mother of three teenage daughters, is sure this problem centers on her husband, John, a consulting architect who travels a great deal. Joan is outraged because he is having an affair with a Christian woman active in her local church who has two sons.

Mid-Life Crisis?

To get a more balanced view of the situation, I arranged an appointment with John. Initially he insisted on dismissing his long tryst with Allison as a mid-life crisis. "After all, everybody goes through these crises nowadays," he offered. "I have a right to do something for myself," he mused. "It's just one of those things."

"John, you're a Christian, not the subject of a mid-life crisis," I countered. "There's more going on than hormones. Is this only a fling? Or do you and Joan have some problems at home?" With little hesitation John recited accumulated grievances about his wife's domineering coldness, how she makes him feel inadequate and how he seems never able to please her. He sees himself as passive and unable to stand against Joan's verbal and emotional quickness. He has resigned himself to an aura of sadness and quiet desperation. He sees his redeeming feature as his love for his children.

John is torn. He's not sure he wants out of the marriage, but for now his fling is very fulfilling. He realizes that far deeper needs than sexual ones are being satisfied, even at the risk of his marriage. He also admits unhappily that he will perhaps never be able to meet his wife's demands. John knows that if it were not for his three daughters, leaving the marriage would be easier.

John and Joan agreed to meet with me and at least talk about the marriage and a possible divorce. Joan is adamant that adultery, and John in committing it, are totally wrong. She denies any fault in the matter. John, while intellectually admitting adultery is wrong, chooses not to buckle under Joan's harangues. He has finally found one thing Joan cannot control, his relationship with Allison.

The problem is simple and painful. Joan still loves John and wants him back, but John, for the first time in his life, has discovered a power by which he can stand against Joan's domination. Adultery is sin, but so is Joan's self-righteous and uncompromising attitude toward him.

Joan's response to their deadlock was predictable. "I'm right. He's wrong!" Her confidence in her sexual fidelity exonerated her of any wrong-doing and obscured another deadlock: might she have done something to drive John into Allison's arms?

Joan thinks she knows the solution: John must take total responsibility for their problems. Initially Joan came to me as a minister to win moral support against John. But from a scriptural perspective, an appeal to one's sinless self-righteousness is as wrong as adultery. As long as Joan maintains her total innocence and her husband's total guilt, she will not be willing to understand herself and John as human beings confronting a faltering marriage together, shrouded in moral compromise. Joan appeals to her godly self-righteousness. But her real appeal is to the myth that adultery is the only sin. This leads her to condemn and reject John instead of pursuing the heart of their problem.

A more realistic solution is for John to end his affair with Allison. Joan needs to end her affair with self-righteousness. Joan has been sexually faithful, but she bears some responsibility for her difficulties. Joan will have to become less overpowering and demanding in the relationship; John will have to become stronger in his relationships with Allison, Joan and himself and quit running away.

Wounded Pride

Different issues come into play over Ralph's affair with Evelyn, his wife Cindy's high school classmate. Cindy's pride is more wounded than anything, and she is further repulsed because she considers her rival to be social, spiritual and physical trash.

Evelyn comes from a poor family and she will never make the cover of *Vogue*. "If Ralph had to have an affair, why couldn't he pick a better woman!" Cindy avers. Good point at the surface level. The reason many Christians who have affairs do so with lovers who are less attractive, less socially sophisticated and who already live unhappy lives is because they feel guilty. They want to be found out and opt for self-destructive rather than liberating behavior.

Cindy parades her sacrifices for the family: her work, her loss of a promising career to raise the children and her support of Ralph. Her self-portrait is pristine. But under the surface lurks the profile of an angry, arrogant and demanding woman. Cindy takes obvious pride in her fashionable clothing, polished social graces and expensive tastes.

Obviously, Ralph's behavior is wrong. But Cindy considers him wrong not so much because he has betrayed their marriage vows, but because he chose an unattractive woman by Cindy's standards. In doing so he has violated her taste and her sense of propriety. However, in his adulterous protest, Ralph is trying to say to himself and to his wife that beauty, spirituality and social graces are more than skin deep.

Moral Purity and Self-righteousness

The Christian who appeals to moral purity and self-righteousness is often making a thinly disguised appeal to one's own selfishness and self-centeredness. The purifying of the relationship and learning as a couple to become one under the lordship of Jesus Christ are not the first problems to be solved. The real difficulties arise because self-centeredness and self-righteousness claim center stage and prevent reconciliation.

In these situations, both women I described have turned moral advantage away from affecting reconciliation and therefore have inflicted deeper wounds. Jumping on a band wagon of self-righteousness is a tempting sin for many Christians. The result is often a roughshod romp over a marital problem that *leads to* the adultery. The situation is made worse and there is no healing.

The shoe fits on the other spiritual foot as well. Christian wives also engage in adulterous relationships, and the potential for the husband to self-righteously deny responsibility for the affair exists too.

Note the case of Glenda, whose husband, Tom, often works a late shift, leaving her to spend lonely hours at home. Glenda's involvement with James began innocently encough one afternoon when he walked into her office and noticed her crying. Kind, comforting and caring, James waited for Tom's next stretch of night-shift duty to begin his sexual midnight express with Glenda.

Eventually Tom found out and confronted Glenda. Filled with emotional and spiritual remorse, she repented. They are having weekly counseling sessions with their pastor to help restore the marriage, and Glenda has set aside her impulsive way of dealing with lonliness. In part because Tom dropped his initial self-righteous anger, Glenda and Tom have realized that their marriage is more important than her fidelity. Tom is also renewing his commitment to spend quality time with Linda when he works the night shift.

Legalism Creates Battle Lines

The Scripture is uncompromising in its teachings on marital fidelity. Sons and daughters are to leave mothers and fathers, to select/be selected as a partner for marriage "until death us do part." The teaching of marital fidelity is the core of the family, which in turn was the basis of social organization for ancient Israel and the foundation for the New Testament church. Marital fidelity is also the standard against which all other human relations are measured. Fidelity and loving actions are the witness of Job, The Song of Solomon, The Psalms, Hosea and many of the biblical illustrations of covenant keeping.

But faithfulness is more than strictly following proscribed rules of behavior. That is mere legalism, and it creates battle lines that produce the deadlock of adultery. I have defined two types of such legalistic behavior.

The Bible Says...

In Matthew 5:32 Jesus offers a teaching that receives considerable attention: "But I tell you that anyone who divorces his wife, except for marital unfaithfulness, causes her to become an adulteress; and anyone who marries the divorced woman commits adultery."

This and other passages declare that adultery is *prima-facie* evidence and justification for divorce. To be involved in an adulterous relationship is the paramount sin against marriage. We must realize that adultery is more than a feeling or an attitude. It is a highly intentional behavior, and any reasonable person knows whether she or he has committed adultery. A problem arises when the offended party appeals to key biblical teachings against adultery and uses the Bible as a legalistic bludgeon. This scriptural beating makes genuine reconciliation unlikely. When ultimatums are used, the terms of settlement don't last long.

The Bible takes a clear stand that adultery is wrong; judgment must be exacted. But God did not *destroy* King David because of his affair with Bathsheba. David had the moral courage to repent because the prophet Nathan led him into repentance. But Nathan did not begin with a frontal, moralistic attack (2 Samuel 11-12). Legalistic ultimatums squeeze the life out of a relationship. One may obtain a moral victory and gain total submission. But one may also have quenched the Spirit. Scoring debate points in an argument over what the Bible says may win an argument, but it may not win the relationship.

My Spouse is My Property

A common ancient world view holds that a wife has no more status than land, cattle, sheep or goats. The gospel brings a new view of reality: there is neither male nor female, free nor slave, Jew nor Gentile. One does not own another.

Many men justify their adulterous escapades on the premise that, "My wife is my property. I can do what I please with her." In the jurisprudence of Western civilization, that attitude cannot be supported. An appeal to a legalistic abuse of one's spouse is an appeal to a distorted, popular myth of ownership and is neither biblical nor Christian.

To view one's husband or wife as an individual possession is not the foundation of a good marriage. We do not possess a marriage relationship or a partner. We *are* the marriage relationship. To act as a possessor of a spouse is to be guided solely by self-interest. Where legalism abounds, battle lines are drawn, deadlocks formed. One may win a legalistic battle but lose the spiritual war.

A cure for this kind of legalism is to remember that we have *all* sinned and fallen short of the glory of God. Think, too, of Jesus' observation that anyone who entertains lustful thoughts toward another has already committed adultery in his or her mind. While a person may never have been physically unfaithful to the marriage partner, scriptural prohibitions go beyond the obvious act.

All Have Sinned

One recalls President Jimmy Carter's *Playboy* magazine interview a number of years ago. As a born-again Christian, Carter spoke of having sexual fantasies, if not outright sexual lust. *Playboy* made money on the President's comments, and Carter suffered from them. As a result, many evangelical Christians drove their sexual fantasies further underground. The moral outrage by the self-righteous guardians of the faith that no born-again Christian—President of the United States or not—dare have any sexual tinge to his moral character was overpowering.

In recent years the Christian community has been even more embarrassed by the sexual escapades of television evangelists. But none of this should come as a complete surprise. Human beings are created with sexual impulses, energies and desires. To cite the scriptural admonition (Matthew 5:27-28) as a rationale for never having a sexual thought outside sexual intercourse with one's husband or wife is to misinterpret Scripture. Jesus was teaching against *dwelling* on sexual thoughts, of being obsessed by, and addicted to, sexual fantasies. In light of Jesus' teachings, one might agree that President Carter showed moral courage to speak of his sexual fantasies.

Sexual energies are processed if we recognize them, acknowledge them and release them in constructive ways. Otherwise they become demons that possess and drive us deeper into aberrations of spiritual and social misconduct.

An appeal to self-righteousness in the face of someone else's adultery is inappropriate. If we believe Romans 3:23, that "all have sinned and fall short of the glory of God," then no one can make a categorical statement, "I would never commit adultery." From the beginning Adam and Eve were fully capable of the sin they committed. They had free will.

We cannot control what our imaginations offer. But we can control how we act on them. We set ourselves up for denial, out-of-control behavior or various forms of moral and sexual confusion by protesting too loudly, "*I* would never commit adultery."

If It Happens

Sexual adultery happens all too frequently. In some cases people claim they are justified. But when adultery occurs, the partners must do three things to put the marriage back on track.

1. Mutual Repentance

Each party must repent of his or her part in the adulterous relationship. One spouse may believe he or she was driven into an affair because the partner has withdrawn from him or her. One may enter into an affair out of neglect or revenge. But no matter which spouse committed adultery, both share in the guilt, and both are called to repent. Repentance must be mutual and shared face to face!

2. Mutual Forgiveness

By the same token, as each partner faces and confronts the other, both husband and wife must be willing to offer *and* receive forgiveness from the other. Neither is without sin. No marriage partner stands in perfect, moral purity, isolated from the sinful behavior of the spouse. If forgiveness cannot be granted, then self-righteousness will prevail, and the relationship reverts to accused and accuser.

3. Mutual Exchange of Marriage Vows

Once mutual repentance has been offered and mutual forgiveness exchanged, then the time comes for the pastor to offer the couple a renewal service to re-dedicate the marriage and make a commitment to the future.

Unless mutual repentance, forgiveness and exchange of vows occur, the adultery syndrome will not be broken.

Emotional Adultery

It is also important to recognize that sexual adultery is not the only way of being unfaithful in marriage relationships. There also exists a kind of emotional adultery in which people place possessions, job, recreation or simply self-interest ahead of their spouses.

From all outward appearances Tim is the model Christian husband. Active in Full Gospel Businessmen's Association, he found meaningful fellowship there following his conversion. He is a cross-country trucker and was previously accustomed to motels, drinking and a wild life. Tim is happy and secure now in his spiritual life with his men's prayer breakfasts. Three times weekly you can spot his car parked at the truck stop off the interstate highway, meeting with his friends for prayer and thanksgiving. But for Alice, his wife, life has not really changed. When Tim was on the road carousing, she was left at home alone, without a breakfast companion; without a sensitive, warm, loving bedroom companion; without someone to share her life, including responsibilities for their three teenage children. Tim is not involved in sexual misconduct at the prayer breakfasts. But he has spiritually violated the covenant of fidelity between them because he has transferred his energies and interests from motel bedrooms to motel dining rooms.

Adultery of the heart is misplacing what should be central in one's life. Tim has found the right place for his heart in his salvation. However, his human relationships must become more mature. Only when he breaks this adultery of the heart will Alice and the children know that Tim is a faithful husband and father, a true man of God.

Carol's heart of adultery also manifests itself in her excessive "spiritual" activities. Her husband is a hard worker. He holds a regular job and moonlights by selling products from his woodworking hobby. Most evenings and weekends Bob is busy either at work or on the road with his wares at art and craft shows. He scarcely finds time for Carol and the children.

An active member of a local church, Carol has become involved in the Wednesday morning prayer group. She is motivated by loneliness and a spiritual quest. But if one were to eavesdrop on her group's typical two and one-half hour sessions, one would observe more than a Bible study. Peeling back the layers of spiritual language, one discovers a well-organized gossip ring. Prayer requests amount to little more than tid-bits of local rumors. Once an hour-long Bible study session, this group has degenerated into a morning-long brunch, with Bibles closed for the most part. The group's focus has become gossip, not God's Word.

Carol would be the first to deny that her Wednesday morning coffee klatch is in any way an adulterous relationship. But ask Bob. When he comes home at night—and often he should be home earlier—Carol is either on the phone to her groupie friends or preparing Bible study materials or resting from her labors. Clearly she is violating her faithfulness both to her husband and to the intent of the Bible studies.

Frances is the middle-aged wife of a successful, and therefore busy, surgeon in a county seat town. Paul chose to settle in this town years ago because he could be the chief cook and bottle washer when it came to surgery. His days are filled with surgical procedures, visiting patients and being the "campus hero" at the hospital. Paul is hardly ever home before 8:00 p.m. and always at work by 7:30 in the morning. As a result, Paul and Frances' marriage is on a rocky road. In talking to her pastor about her distress, Frances remarked that, "His work is his mistress!" How true. Paul is married to his work. His wife and three children have been orphaned by his success. They are crushed by the accolades community and hospital staff frequently bestow upon him. Adultery of the heart? You bet! What turns Paul on is his work, not his family.

These are not the only forms of emotional adultery. One may repeatedly place her mother, his children, her education, his racquetball club or her church ahead of the marriage, frequently leading to wedlock deadlock.

Emotional adultery occurs more frequently than sexual adultery and is usually more subtle. Changes in attitudes and spiritual maturity can break the heart adultery as well as the physical adultery patterns.

Christian Truth:
But the Fruit of the Spirit is . . .

Wedlock deadlock involving sexual and emotional adultery can be overcome. Scripture defines the characteristics of maturity in Christ. They are listed in Galatians 5:16-23 as the fruit of the Spirit: love, joy, peace, patience, kindness, goodness, faithfulness, gentleness and self-control. Cultivating this fruit builds maturity and helps us deal with selfishness, unwillingness to change and other destructive attitudes.

As we learn to be led by the Spirit (Galatians 5:19) we develop Christlike attitudes that break wedlock deadlock. Following are five "Nos" that should be adopted to maintain a healthy perspective.

No Spitefulness

Because a partner has betrayed another through adultery, resentment, scheming and retaliation can result. Vengeful attitudes are very self-destructive and are not good correctives for the situation.

Glen, a successful attorney, works long hours. His frequent absence from home seemed routine to Linda. As she now reflects upon the three years before Glen left her, she realizes that he had been coming home later and later. He would withdraw into evening silence and leave earlier in the morning. His explanation was simple: he needed morning exercise to cope with job stress that required him to work late at the office. He offered less and less of himself to his family.

Then came the announcement. For at least two years Glen had been involved with another woman. One morning, he stayed home late enough to tell Linda he was moving out. They never had an ugly fight. Both were active in their local Presbyterian church, he an elder and she chairperson of the education committee. From Linda's viewpoint, she had been wronged by Glen's deceptive and adulterous behavior. Reaching that conclusion, she could have jumped on a moral soap box to rant and rave.

However, as she talked to her counselor, she began to realize that Glen had controlled and deceived her long enough. It would not benefit her now to permit these negatives to control the rest of her life. She resolved to continue in her church activities, stay with her prayer partners and remain active in her community volunteer work.

Even though Glen had walked out on her, Linda remained considerate of him despite his marital betrayal of her and his abandonment of their two adolescent sons. Spite would not get the best of her even under circumstances that morally had already become ugly. She chose the high road instead of becoming defeated and paralyzed by her partner's sin.

No Arguing

People in conflict seem to draw others quickly and boisterously into arguments that often are pointless, alienating and destructive. Leigh is a strong-willed woman who frequently argues with her husband. She complains bitterly that he hurts her by his impulsive spending, insensitive remarks and sarcastic commentary. Leigh is learning to be led by the Spirit by going beyond using her own hurt as a trading item to get her husband to give her what she wants.

No Salt-Pouring

A good friend, especially a marriage partner, shares certain vulnerabilities and sensitivities that are carefully guarded. Sharing these intimacies makes us vulnerable. Learning to be led by the spirit encourages us to learn to love spontaneously. We learn to love by helping and encouraging. We learn not to pour salt in the open wounds of our partners and take advantage of vulnerable areas.

No Vague Promises

Ben had been a four-star student in college and law school, and his career seemed equally destined for those stars. Donna was a shrewd and perceptive "career scout." She picked an economic winner. Ben had become professionally wealthy. Donna admitted to her pastor that her motives for marriage were selfish and economically ruthless. Eventually Ben realized Donna had married for money, not for a mate.

Nominal church goers, Ben and Donna apparently had sensed the mutual emptiness and unhappiness in their lives and agreed to attend a revival series at a church. Both made serious commitments to Christ to reorder their lives. Howeverm still fearful that Donna would take him to the cleaners, Ben was unwilling to share the strategy and details of his investment portfolio and long-term plans, especially any plans to return a full measure of his money to the Lord.

Ben had promised Donna that if she would honor him instead of his dollars, he would share more of his income and plans with her. As a new child of God, he would be nicer to her and would resume the family domestic and spiritual leadership. Donna wanted a new and revised Ben. But as sensitive as she tried to be in encouraging Ben to be open and honest about his income—its source, its flow, its goal—Ben's promises remained characteristically elusive and vague.

To be led by the Spirit is to invite the Holy Spirit to lead both husband and wife to be accountable to each other. Let your yes be yes; let your no be no. Ben's income level mattered less to Donna than his commitment to be responsible. What Ben needed from Donna was her faithfulness in pursuing him, not his career. Made in the mutuality of love, promises of fiscal and marital fidelity in all the details of life will follow. Mutual faithfulness is a fruit of the Spirit.

No Self-Righteous Rage

Linda had every moral and spiritual motivation for jumping on a soap box to spread self-righteous rage throughout the earth: Glen had betrayed her. But in Christ she chose not to do that. She had come to realize, with a rare and sensitive degree of maturity, that we all disappoint each other. The mark of spiritual maturity is to press on and not lapse into self-righteous and self-serving rage.

Still, it is not enough to say "no" at the appropriate time. We must allow the Holy Spirit to grow the fruit of the Spirit in our lives. And that takes God's grace in our lives, the origin of which transcends human motives. It is only and finally God's love and God's grace. There is a harvest of the Spirit to sow and to reap.

1. Love

We have high expectations for people we love. We want them to fulfill those expectations. To love, in the deepest and most profound sense of the word, means to risk a great deal. To risk is to take initiative, to step out and to sacrifice for someone else. Love is not easy. It is a high risk activity.

George had vastly overextended himself in business loans, especially bank notes to cover his secretive involvement in a sales networking scheme. After several thousands of dollars had disappeared with no return in sight, George became depressed and uncharacteristically withdrawn from his wife, Delores. Following a tearful and prayerful time of mutual confession, Delores offered—out of love for George—to take an extra job to pay back the bank notes. She didn't want either a divorce or a depressed husband. She had no motivation but love for George and his happiness. Delores' second-job and second-mile paychecks were gladly harvested by this couple together as a fruit of the Spirit—long-suffering love.

2. Joy

Motivate with a smile. We hear a lot about body language and negative communication through tone, looks and even manner of dress. To live with joy is to offer an affectionate smile in all that you do, in the simple chores and joyous happenings of life. Joy is contagious. Offer it often.

We are commanded by God's word to rejoice in all things. To fulfill this commandment in the fruit of joy means beginning each day with a word of thanksgiving and praise, first to God, then to the marriage partner. Joy, as a fruit of the Spirit, is seen in the early-morning thankfulness for the gift of a spouse and the gift of life that keeps the marriage from getting up on the wrong side of the bed.

3. Peace

Many husbands and wives who work outside the home long to return after work and experience peace at last. Home should be a place of rest and sanctuary. One way to have a "night cap" of peace at home is spending quality time with the children and with the spouse. Once children are in bed, time needs to be set aside for a "peace conference" and sensuous peace making between husband and wife. A loving marriage relationship produces the fruit of peace in the late evening hours of sweet solitude between husband and wife.

4. Patience

Many men I know readily admit to being impatient, especially if it means going shopping with their wives. A maturity developed by the Holy Spirit enables a person to accept that some aspects of your relationship with your spouse may never be fun or pass quickly. As in another example, the husband may be a neat-nick, the wife a free spirit. When angry, she may accuse him of being a rigid perfectionist, and he will countercharge that she is a living slob. Patience is the fruit of the Spirit that allows one to enjoy, even in conflict, the unique gifts that the other personality brings, whether at home or in the shopping mall.

5. Kindness

We need to learn to use restraint. There's no room for spiteful behavior in the Christian marriage. Jennifer is married to Scott, a high-powered executive. She is easily wounded in spirit by his managerial abrasiveness. During the course of their marriage, she began carrying a spiritual gunnysack filled with Scott's aggressive sins. If this marriage is to be successful and bear the fruit of the Spirit, Jennifer will have to dump the gunnysack and fill it with kindness. Scott may also need to respond to her kindly. Scott doesn't receive or give much kindness at work. In his work world, one can lose a contract or a job if one blinks. Scott's relentless concentration on his goals cuts no slack. How wonderful for Scott and Jennifer to empty the gunnysack of slights and relax enough with each other to blink and rediscover the delightful twinkle in each other's eyes. In that playful twinkle of the eye, one sees kindness, the delightful fruit of the Spirit.

6. Goodness

Enhancing your partner's well-being creates goodness. Gail and Alex had been married for years. Alex had been abandoned by his mother when he was a young boy, but years later his mother managed to locate Alex. Gail had serious misgivings about what might happen in a mother-son reunion. However, she offered Alex the gift of goodness and encouraged him to meet with his mother after a forty-year break. A big risk? Yes! But the goodness of his Spirit overcomes the risk. The reunion occurred, and blessed by Gail's gift of goodness, Alex could bless his wayward mother and return, eternally thankful, to Gail, God's gift to him.

7. Faithfulness

Plan to be there for your spouse and your family whenever possible. It may be a ball game or the bedroom, a church retreat or a scout meeting. Faithfulness includes sexual faithfulness, but at a deeper level it is a covenant faithfulness to the marriage relationship in all areas of life.

Tom, a classic workaholic, spends seventy to eighty hours on the job. Married relatively late in life, this is his second and his wife's first marriage. Although Sandy has a successful career, she is eager to start a family and desperate for a more active sexual relationship with Tom. Deeply religious, Sandy remained a virgin until their marriage. She looked forward to the marriage and raising children. But Tom cannot break himself away from work long enough, according to Sandy, even to have sex. At a philosophical level, he insists he wants children, but he never comes home in time! Work captivates his heart and absorbs his energy while Sandy awaits him in their bedroom. Tom needs to receive the fruit of Sandy's faithfulness and offer faithful parenthood to his marriage.

8. Gentleness

Encourage and nurture each other. Gwen had been sexually abused as a child and was overly concerned and sensitive to the interactions between her husband and their infant son. Fearful that Rob might engage in some sexual exploitation toward their son, Gwen went through a difficult period in which she surrendered gentleness. After talking to a counselor for several sessions, she began to realize that the nurture between Rob and their son was healthy and normal. In turn, Rob was able to nurture her into greater strength in their relationship.

9. Self-control

This means far more than keeping one's temper. In families it means letting go of the children and learning to grow as a parent. Self-control means taking care of some of your spouse's needs to share time together. Self-control means not slipping into the easy routine of watching television or reading the paper or magazines every evening and not letting either temper or other people control all that you do.

Self-control involves keeping natural instincts of ill temper or passivity toward your family sacrificially under wraps as a gift of God through you to your spouse.

In Sum

To commit adultery or to have an adulterous relationship arise against you as the innocent party is a blight and curse upon the marriage. For the marriage to continue, the adulterous relationship and motive must be exorcised. The adultery of the body can be identified, located and destroyed if both husband and wife agree.

Adultery of the heart, however, is not a physical act and may be more difficult to exorcise. Confession of adultery of the heart has to be subtle, because it is a confession of an attitude.

The successful and rewarding Christian marriage must be built on sexual fidelity. But the deeper reality is not one of bodily fidelity alone, but of a fidelity of spirit. Not engaging in adultery for the Christian is but a partial truth of the gospel. The full truth is found in the fruit of the Spirit.

Out of self-restraint and out of the spiritual, loving constraint for one's spouse, the Christian is called upon to fulfill both the letter and the spirit of marital unity and fidelity.

The wedlock conflict of whether one partner or the other is committing adultery of body or attitude can only be overcome by the fruit of the Spirit. The wonderful thing about bearing the fruit of God's Holy Spirit in marriage is that it can be seen, felt and experienced. Marital deadlocks are put asunder and Christian growth united when marriage partners look beyond what they dare not do, to what they dare risk for each other. Then the whole world knows we are Christians by our love *and* the marital fruit of the Spirit.

Two

But I've Held the Marriage Together

Popular Myth:
My Leadership Keeps the Family Together

Christian Truth:
Submission Is not One-Way; It Is Mutual

Popular Myth:
My Leadership Keeps the Family Together

Submission and spiritual leadership have formed a hot potato of sorts for the church. One of the most familiar passages on the subject is found in Ephesians:

> Submit to one another out of reverence for Christ. Wives, submit to your husbands as to the Lord. For the husband is the head of the wife as Christ is the head of the church . . . Husbands, love your wives, just as Christ loved the church and gave himself up for her . . . In this same way, husbands ought to love their wives as their own bodies. He who loves his wife loves himself. After all, no one ever hated his own body, but he feeds and cares for it, just as Christ does the church—for we are members of his body (Ephesians 5:21-23, 25, 28-30).

Some of the more traditional teachings of verse 22 ("Wives submit to your husbands as to the Lord") demand that women be totally subservient to their husbands. The claim is that the husband is head of the household, and he rules the women (wife and daughters and daughters-in-law) in his household with absolute authority.

Women, therefore, have been taught that their goal—if not ambition—in life is to submit to the husband as though he were the Lord Jesus Christ himself. That sort of authority, given and claimed, frequently leads to abusive behavior by the husband. He believes his "lordship" gives him unrestrained sexual access to his wife, as well as complete authority over her emotionally and fiscally.

However, a careful reading of the passage clearly places an even greater responsibility on the husband. In Ephesians 5:25, the apostle Paul's words are absolutely clear: "Husbands, love your wives, just as Christ loved the church and gave himself up for her." Wives are not asked to give up their lives for their husbands, but husbands are. The church would not have come into being had Jesus not taken the *loving initiative* to submit himself sacrificially to a church that did not yet exist.

Therefore, according to this passage, the husband is to take the initiative not to demand submission. Rather, out of loving support, he must be willing to give up his life *first* for his wife and family. The husband's authority in the household, if we are to take Jesus seriously, is not based on the wife's initial submission to him but on the husband's loving, sacrificial submission out of love for his wife.

We are also called to *mutual submission,* not as a combative or competitive stalemate, but out of our mutual, spiritual submission to Jesus Christ. We submit willingly and lovingly to one another not out of mutual demands but out of mutual *reverence for Christ* (Ephesians 5:21).

God can't force us to submit willingly, lovingly and reverentially. That would be tyrannical. Ultimately God can only invite us to share the blessings of mutual submission, first to Jesus as Lord and then to one another as members of the household of faith.

He Must Be My Kind of Leader

Unfortunately, because of a misunderstanding of this passage, a popular myth circulating among Christian women is that by forcing their husbands to become the heads of their households they will hold the marriage together. Often the women most afflicted with this notion are type A personalities (aggressive, high-achieving) married to type B men (relaxed, easy-going). These couples must learn that the foundation of a successful marriage is built upon principles of mutual respect, trust and love. Being the spiritual head of a household is more profound and subtle than being socially aggressive and spiritually competitive.

Cher and Max demonstrate a classic example of this kind of deadlock. Cher called my office to make an appointment for Max, who dutifully and willingly showed up with a smile. He sketched for me the marital deadlock between them, including his love for Cher, his unwavering commitment to the marriage and his desire to make the relationship better. From both Max's story and Cher's eventual involvement in joint counseling sessions, I realized that the central problem in their marriage was spiritual. Cher is angry because Max refuses to yield to a popular spiritual myth about family leadership; he won't offer the spiritual leadership she had envisioned.

The challenge in this marriage is twofold. Cher must develop a more mature understanding of spiritual leadership, and Max must be more honest and assertive as a husband and head of the household. The fundamental changes required for this marriage to break out of its wedlock deadlock are, above all, spiritual. Then attitudinal and behavioral changes will follow. The core of our being is spiritual, not psychological. To be a spiritual leader, the husband doesn't have to be a type A personality. The test of Cher's faith is that Max can be an effective spiritual leader without being type A.

Arbitrary Leadership

When Buddy and Joyce came to see me about their marriage, each gave different reasons for their problems. Buddy asserted his authority as head of the household. He was angry with his wife because she refused to do everything he told her to do. Joyce said she wanted Buddy to be the head of the family, but that Buddy claimed his authority in self-serving, arbitrary and capricious ways. She said he wanted to be head of the house when it suited him, but not on days when he was depressed, in a bad mood or wanted Joyce to take care of petty details. I realized that Buddy had initiated the counseling because he wanted me, as a male, to take his side.

This wedlock deadlock is the flip side of Max and Cher's problem. Joyce is much too willing to be passive and totally compliant. Buddy is immature and inconsistent about how and under what circumstances he chooses to be both spiritual and relational head of the household. By assuming what he believes to be strong leadership, Buddy thinks he's holding his marriage together and making it work effectively. Cher, on the other hand, is convinced that Max has abdicated his responsibilities, forcing her into leadership. Cher persistently insists that Max must fit her ideal mode of a leader.

Cher is gifted with a strong, articulate and aggressive personality. That's one reason Max fell in love with her. She is very bright and wants things done right—immediately. She is overly eager for her husband, her children, her employer, her pastor and anyone else who crosses her path to conform to her ideal of success. Often her behavior alienates the people she loves the most and who could best help her.

Like Buddy, Cher feels her leadership style is the only possible one that will hold the marriage together. But to strengthen her relationship with Max, Cher will have to rein in her personality. She must accept the fact that those around her simply are not as aggressive as she. Cher must know too that manipulating Max and others to conform to her spiritual projections of God's will for them won't work. In both cases, all partners must learn to relate better to the other's personalities if they hope to develop mature marriages.

Power Leadership

Sometimes people will assume leadership if it is power on their terms. This sort of forceful spiritual leadership, when used to keep the family on the right track, can also lead to wedlock deadlock. In the Evans family the mere mention of anything of a spiritual or theological bent evokes a running commentary from Rachel about how one's life can be spiritually improved. Earlier in the marriage her spiritual critiques may have provided pleasant and congenial analyses of church events, Sunday school class discussions and the Sunday morning sermon. Now her comments are uninvited and have become a source of divisiveness and rancor within the family. They are no longer spiritually instructive or emotionally constructive.

Rachel's concern that her children grow up instructed in the way of the Lord has become an obsession: any comment, image or illustration arising in family religious discussions becomes a launching pad for her sermons. Her commentaries are broken records and old tapes, according to her family. Billy, her husband, and their three children perceive Rachel as interfering, moralistic and judgmental. That's not what she wants, but that's the fallout from her attitude that everyone must be her kind of Christian. To exercise spiritual leadership, she must be sensitive to her family's needs and not bludgeon them with her ideals.

Passive Leadership

Russ exemplifies a more passive style of leadership. He and Maxine have been married for more than twenty-five years, are active in their church and have a son, now in college. Each has a successful career. Over the years Russ has convinced himself that he needs a tremendous amount of privacy. He must have his own bedroom, although he and Maxine enjoy good sex and each other's company. It's common knowledge to family or guests that Russ cannot be disturbed during his television evening news "worship service." On weekends you can spot his car at the local doughnut shop, the same one where he stops each day on his way to work *and* on his way home. Maxine complains vigorously that Russ totally abdicates his leadership as husband and father. His retort is unwavering. He says he has to have his privacy, doughnuts and coffee.

At the bottom of the conflict lies Russ' idea that life has to be played by his rules. If Maxine dares to complain or if son Robert asks him to be more involved with the family, Russ retreats into his speech about his "quiet time." Russ' uncompromising rules are like a downhill runaway truck, continually picking up momentum, rolling out of control.

Maxine and Robert are in revolt. Russ' rules permit him to do whatever he wants but prohibit his wife and son from making any demands on him. Russ insists on being his kind of leader. It is true that everyone needs solace, privacy and time for personal rejuvenation. However, Christian truth does not allow Russ' privacy to come at the expense of rejecting his responsibilities for his family, including private time for his son and his wife. Russ has not offered true Christian leadership for himself or his family.

Total Control

Buddy and Joyce struggle because he insists on having total control of the family, including Joyce's paycheck. There is no mutuality because he believes the man controls the money. Buddy considers financial control as being interchangeable with his identity. He defends himself by alleging that Joyce does not spend money wisely. Joyce admits she isn't as financially prudent as Buddy, and he says he holds the marriage together through managing money. Their deadlock can only be broken if Buddy is willing to submit to joint accountability. Otherwise his claim that his shrewd fiscal policies hold the marriage together will indeed be scattered on unfruitful, rocky ground.

Kristen married Rick late in life after achieving career success. Before marrying she enjoyed a good social life and making money. Kristen decided she had been a single woman in the work force long enough; she had paid her dues. Marriage meant quitting work and enjoying nesting. However, Kristen is puzzled by Rick's anger at her decision.

Their marriage won't collapse without Kristen's income, but Rick planned on a bigger house, a better second car and nicer vacation trips, based on a dual income. Kristen's loss of income destroyed that pipe dream, but she still talks about extravagant vacations, big parties, a large house and a sports car. She won't go to work, and hubby can't hold the marriage and their dreams together with his fiscal leadership and paycheck. Kristen and Rick have a classic wedlock deadlock. Two cannot live more extravagantly than one on a single income. If Kristen is to realize all the benefits she believes she's entitled to in her marriage, she's going to have to submit to the authority of the work place to make money to finance her marital dreams.

Fiscal Independence

A refusal to submit to fiscal interdependence often leads to deadlock. Phil works hard as a construction foreman. He makes good money, enjoys excellent health, loves his wife, Wilma, and is committed to his marriage. Phil, now in his mid-forties, knows his income won't change much, except for routine increases in pay. Wilma's father is a retired successful businessman who has already given three of his four children substantial monies from his sizable estate. Wilma's father is quite capable of caring for himself financially in his retirement. Even though he will probably never require help from his children, Wilma carefully keeps the money given to her by her father in an account separate from family operating expenses.

In a marriage counseling session, Phil complains to his pastor about this strategy. Wilma would agree to a family budget, but she wants the freedom to splurge on gifts and the latest designer fashions. She likes giving graduation, wedding or party gifts and dips into her estate monies for them. Phil realizes Wilma has a generous heart, but he feels betrayed because his wife keeps her funds and spending plans completely secret. He says he is not trying to use her money or override her generosity and social gregariousness. Still, Wilma is fearful that Phil will interfere with her financial plans, and she is not about to give up her independence.

Phil is busy trying to hold the marriage together through his work, his commitment to his wife and his devotion to the church.

His hurt and anger focus on Wilma's inability to trust him enough for them to develop *together* plans for and limits on the use of her estate money. Until Wilma shares her plans with Phil, their marriage will flounder on the ambiguity of who is in charge.

Spiritual Life of Leisure

Anne also insists in maintaining independence rather than helping Neil hold things together. Both of them were employed in well-paying careers before they married. They made a commitment that when children came along Anne would initially give up full-time work and then eventually would work part time. That decision was made some fifteen years ago, before the escalation of child rearing costs and property taxes. In addition, Neil and Anne made a substantial building fund pledge to their local church. Neil volunteers for a considerable amount of overtime in order to supplement the family coffers, and Anne gets angry with him because he is not at home to spend time with her and the children. His weekend is filled either with overtime work or with routine house maintenance. Neil is frustrated because he cannot sit down with Anne and look at the present realities of what it means to have three young, bright, active children who absorb a tremendous amount of time with their various activities.

Neil finally put it this way to Anne, "You're gonna have to give up your spiritual life of leisure. I know you love the church and its activities. I know you love driving the neighborhood kids to church, school, gymnastics and scouting activities. And I want you to have that," he said in a genuinely affirming way. "But," he continued, "we simply cannot make ends meet to do all the things we want to do as a family and to provide opportunities for our children unless you are willing either to cut back on yours or the children's activities. Or, you can go to work full time to produce more income to help support family commitments."

Anne, however, would not hear of such a compromise. She was not willing to give up her church work, her volunteer committee work and her involvement as classroom mother for her two sons and daughter. Unless Anne gives up some of her independence, Neil will have more and more difficulty trying to hold the marriage together himself.

Finally, when either a husband or wife says, "But I've held the marriage together" there are definite trouble spots. The first sign of trouble occurs when one of the spouses projects onto the more cooperative, less demanding spouse a demand that "You must do things exactly the way I want."

A second trouble spot comes in the stubbornness of saying, as Kristen did, "Yes, I will submit, but it must be on my terms." This flies in the face of mutuality, covenant and personal regard for all family members. Third, living together as husband, wife and family means giving up a larger measure of independence than many care to admit.

Finally, the belief that "*I* have held the marriage together," or insistence that the other partner must hold the marriage together, causes trouble. If the marriage is going to work out it must be by mutual agreement. Otherwise, however positive and strong a spouse's motivation for holding the marriage together, the partner and probably the children will develop a hardness of heart, ill will and a stubborn and uncooperative spirit from the domination implicit in this claim.

Christian Truth:
Submission Is not One-Way; It Is Mutual

Brian and Beverly do not have the typical Christian marriage. When they married they planned to pursue independent careers.

After some ten years of marriage, both were successful. Beverly's job requires her to travel out of town on a fairly regular basis. On the other hand, Brian's work is with a firm in which he works the traditional forty-hour-a-week job. Brian has been supportive of Beverly. But now, as Beverly travels more and makes more money than Brian, he complains loudly about the unappreciated sacrifices he makes for his wife's career. He says he feels used and manipulated.

In listening to Brian and Beverly voice their concerns about the strain in their marriage and Brian's obvious frustration about his sacrifices, it became clear that Brian does not want his wife to be totally submissive. What he does want is respect from Beverly so that he'll know he is appreciated. He wants respect not submission. That's not an unreasonable desire. In fact it's scriptural.

There are four ways in which a marriage can move toward mutual respect instead of demanding arbitrary submission. The parable of the Good Samaritan (Luke 10:29-37) tells us several things about how partners can learn to support one another.

In this story a man was robbed and severely beaten by thieves who left him to die. Two men who saw the injured man passed by on the other side of the road, but the Samaritan helped the victim at his own expense. Just as the Samaritan took the wounded man to the inn, marriage partners must develop the attitude of willingly ministering to a wounded spouse. First, this means that the spouse must find in the other a *companion* willing to share his or her hurts and frustrations.

Second, as the Samaritan and the Jew traveled down the road, a sense of *closeness* developed between them. They were committed to the trip and to a common goal. So must marriage partners work toward that common goal.

A third element is *continuity*. Having decided to go to the inn, neither abandoned the other. Neither was diverted from the path and neither wanted to turn back.

A fourth principle that can be applied to the marriage is *cooperation*. The Good Samaritan could not have taken an uncooperative victim for help. The victim had to be willing to go along if both were to arrive at their desired destination.

In the same way, we are called to be marital Good Samaritans. The roles may well reverse from one time to another. On one day or at one time in life the husband may be the Good Samaritan; and at other times and on other days the wife may be the Good Samaritan. But we are each called to that role for the spouse. On the days when one spouse is the man "left for dead," that partner should be as companionable and cooperative as possible to a spouse who is trying to move the marriage forward through very difficult times.

The theme of the Good Samaritan was more than befriending a beaten stranger. The goal is several fold—to arrive at the same destination, to travel through the difficult times and receive a blessing at the inn of one's life. This drama means that one must be willing and able to be the Good Samaritan, and correspondingly, a spouse must be willing to allow the other spouse to help.

The Good Shepherd

We are also called to be a good shepherd (Psalm 23) in our marriages. The good shepherd prepares a *place* for the sheep, a place of safety and comfort. Jim and Peggy are learning to apply this Psalm to their marriage. Married fifteen years, their first five years were difficult because Peggy was helping Jim through his graduate school program. Eventually Jim's life settled into his career, and in a relatively short span several children were born. Across the years Peggy has become increasingly resentful that she sacrificed her career.

Jim had met with his pastor and several of the elders of his congregation to seek guidance on how to reassure Peggy of his love for her. Their advice was to prepare a place for his wife and family. They needed time for family outings, picnics and going to church together. Further, Jim needed to reassure Peggy that he, as the shepherd, the head of house, wanted a place where they all could be nourished and nurtured. Being the good shepherd is a calling to prepare a place for other family members where they can be secure in their emotional, spiritual and physical needs.

The call to be a good shepherd in the marriage is not only a call to lie down in green pastures around cool and still waters. It is also a call to share *pain*, to go through the valleys of the shadow of death as they loom over a marriage, threatening it with extinction. Often those valleys are more subtle than death itself. They may represent financial responsibilities of putting children through college or facing financial reversals. A marriage may end up in one of these valleys without the couple realizing it because neither partner recognizes the open grave sites.

The good shepherd cannot avoid the valleys. The shadow of death extends its grasp over every life. Still, the good shepherd leads through difficult times, frightening experiences, setbacks, pain and loss. The stalwart, spiritual leadership continues through the suffering until the valleys begin to disappear.

The third important aspect of the good shepherd's ministry is encouraging *peace*. If we are preoccupied with worldly success, finding a perfect home, raising well-behaved children, taking care of everybody's needs, there won't be any peaceful green pastures or still waters in our own household. Encouraging peace takes time, effort and communication.

Finally, the good shepherd leads the family to accept and receive *presence* not possessions. We note that the psalmist has said the goal of life is to dwell in the house of the Lord forever. The good shepherd provides personal presence as head of the household. Many wives and children complain that they don't see the husband or father around the house. They are truly less concerned about possessions than about Dad's availability.

Psalm 23 can be a marital guide in a number of ways. The shepherd does not demand the sheep's submission but invites them, through sensitive leadership, to enjoy the goodness of life, to go through the difficult times, to receive an attitude of peace and to realize that presence with one another is far more important than anything else that might be provided.

Don't Turn Stones into Bread

In another scriptural illustration, I believe we are called to resist changing stones to bread. You will recall that Jesus spent forty days in the wilderness. Seeing his prey hungry and thirsty, Satan's temptation was genuine. Take care of your own needs. Change stones to bread so that you can eat (Matthew 4:1-4). Jesus' resistance was voiced in his teaching, "You shall not live by bread alone." Jesus loved eating and breaking bread. His witness was not that we could not enjoy life. Rather, Jesus resisted the temptation to try to change immediate circumstances to meet his immediate needs instead of thinking of long-term consequences and less obvious needs.

One temptation to change stones to bread is the drive to rescue the wayward spouse. The husband or wife may be having an affair, gambling away time and money, or being overly involved in church, charitable, professional or educational interests. The spouse may need to change. But encouragement to change must be done with delicacy. Forcing the rescue of the wayward spouse is like trying to change stones to bread. A formerly troubled spouse now forced into submissiveness spells trouble for the marriage. The central transformation is an inward one which fosters mutual respect. It cannot be achieved through the passive dependency of a partner rescued by a self-righteous spouse.

Jesus was clearly human when he endured his wilderness temptation. He needed bread, and he needed to renew himself. Making stones into bread would have been an immediate and logical solution. The temptation to change stones to bread in a marriage is to make the husband what the wife wants him to be. At times there may be anger when a wife refuses to be converted from the stone, as the husband perceives her, to a more favorable kind of bread.

One could say that Ruth's husband, Winston, behaves like a classic workaholic. He spends many hours at the office. He is scarcely home except for late-evening meals, and often those are interrupted by business-related phone calls. Ruth is desperate that Winston become the mature Christian he says he is. She has a planned outline for how her husband can be a more solid Christian and a better husband. Ruth has not yet resisted the temptation to turn her stones (Winston) into bread (her image of what he should be). The more she insists in turning her stony husband to bread, the more he will fight being made in her image and the stonier he'll become.

On the other hand, Sid is a delightful and successful salesman. The national organization for which he works rewards his gregarious personality and his technical expertise. Sid's wife, Shelly, does not have a sales-type personality. She works as a computer operator and is modest and shy. Sid's temptation is to turn Shelly into the bread of an aggressive agent. The hardest lesson, perhaps, for Sid to learn is that not everybody is gregarious, aggressive, outgoing and sociable. A shy person may be loving, sustaining, nurturing and respectful. It may be frustrating for Sid not to have the stone of Shelly's shyness turn into the bread of an aggressive sales agent. But he is called to resist trying to transform his wife by some psychological alchemy into someone who is immediately compatible with all his friends and colleagues.

There is a time and a place for everything. Clearly Jesus needed bread to eat, and he enjoyed feasting. But routinely and consistently he resisted the obvious and immediate answer to the challenge of both the devil and his disciples. We may not always be able to rescue our spouses; it may not be best for us to try to make a spouse over in our own image; it may be profoundly unwise for the aggressive, gregarious spouse to try to recreate the partner into a different person.

It will always be difficult for Cher and Anne to submit to authority. Both of these wives are dedicated Christians, love their husbands and want their marriages to succeed. Their frustration is partially because their husbands are not as aggressive, strong and domineering as they are. It would be equally as mistaken for Cher and Anne to try to be quiet and retiring as it would be for Max and Neil to try to be dominating. The issue of how a couple holds a marriage together and how they work out mutual submission when the wife is a more dominating and aggressive personality than the husband is not easy. It certainly cannot be a matter of changing stones to bread. More likely it's going to be a matter of going through the valleys of the shadow of the death of submission and aggressiveness within the family. But the good shepherd is there, and Jesus calls us to resist trying to make bread out of stones when that's not appropriate.

Respect, Not Submission

Strong-willed is strong-willed. Docile personalities are not going to make strong-willed spouses docile. Conversely, strong-willed spouses are not going to make docile people aggressive and strong willed. The truth of the successful marriage under these circumstances is one of learning respect rather than submission under or dominance over the other.

Mutual respect involves learning better pacing, learning to live with the patience level of the other and developing a place for peace in the family. Whether strong-willed or docile, any couple can learn to develop better timing of words and actions, a higher level of patience between them and the goal shared by the Good Samaritan to provide a peaceful place for food, shelter and care. Then the next day's needs can be met.

In Sum

Many have misunderstood the teaching of the Scripture about the wife submitting to the husband as being a natural act. I believe that in many cases where strong-willed Christian women are married, their calling is to be who they are. They are called to choose to submit out of respect for their spouse, as Christ calls us to submit to one another in love. That will not be easy, and it will not be immediate. But it is a possibility that through mutual submission the marriage will flourish. In an attitude of mutual submission, both type A and type B spouses, whether male or female, will be transformed in a unity of spirit—through the fruit of the Holy Spirit. This mutual yielding will transcend their individual personality types and will result in respect, each for the other, that will delightfully surprise everyone.

Three

I Don't Get Sex

Popular Myth:
Marriage Must Always Be Sexy

Christian Truth:
We Do Not Live by Sex Alone

Popular Myth:
Marriage Must Always Be Sexy

Despite AIDS, sex is alive and well in America. The output of R-rated movies, porno literature and the sexually explicit motifs in television miniseries and serials, plus general media advertising, confirm that our society's preoccupation with sex continues to grow. Just as marriages run into financial and emotional deadlocks, they also encounter sexual deadlocks. One of these involves the conflict between the myth that marriage must always be sexy to be good and the deeper truth that we do not live by sex alone. In this chapter, I will explore the issues that relate to developing models for Christian sexuality in marriage.

Max is one example of a Christian who flirts with this myth. He pledged his marital fidelity long ago, and he has honored that commitment. But early in his marriage Max failed to realize that good relationships don't exist by sex alone. He loves sex and enjoys it frequently with his wife, Cher, who is quickly stimulated. Max considers his sexual relationship with Cher like a cup of cold water on a hot summer day—he would like more. But he must realize that cold water, while satisfying and refreshing, cannot be a complete diet. Children, business and career responsibilities come, and one's perspective on life moves beyond the bedroom.

When his buddies brag about their sexual exploits with girlfriends or mistresses, or about the latest sexual technique they've tried with their wives, Max nods appreciatively and somewhat enviously. Max is tempted by the myth that marriage, if it is to be good, must be sexy all the time.

Intense Living

One aspect of our modern mythology about sex is that if one works in a high-tech, high-pressure job, sex and the rest of life must move along with the same degree of intensity. A contradiction in terms? Yes, and that leads to some contradictions that create marital deadlocks.

Kyle, for instance, works in a high-tech environment and supervises a number of employees who spend all day at desk-top computers. A computer wizard himself, Kyle is overly committed to his work, by his own admission and that of his doctor, who prescribes high blood pressure medication.

Several years ago Kyle discovered a secret pleasure. If discreet while walking through the lunchroom or past fellow employees' desks during lunch break, Kyle can enjoy various sexually-oriented magazines and tabloids read by his colleagues. On some days the soft-core fantasies generated by his lunch-hour meanderings jack him up far more than an afternoon cup of coffee with sugar. By the time Kyle arrives home on these days, his fantasies usually have been further stimulated by the popular music tapes in his car tape deck. When he walks through the doorway, he wants his wife, Sarah, to jump out of one of the slick sex magazine's centerfolds. Sarah, however, thinks he is over-sexed. Kyle, who is ready to hit the sack when he hits the front porch, remains convinced that his marriage must always be sexy.

Craig pursues a similar avenue. He's a construction foreman who expends lots of physical energy at work and doesn't have much time for fantasies. His good times come when he's doing a repair job or, ideally, working on a condo unit overlooking a pool flanked by bathing beauties. Some of his soft-porn fantasies are like those of King David who gazed upon the bathing Bathsheba. Kyle and Craig's afternoon fantasies are focused more on the bedroom than on how they might help their wives prepare dinner, clean up the house or go shopping.

A second influence of the computer age on sexual habits is the expectation of immediate gratification. When a computer is "on-line," it means all the equipment is warmed up, ready when the "go" button is tapped. Those ensnared in the popular myth that marriage must always be sexy live with the on-line sexual fantasy, "My spouse is plugged in, warmed up, programmed for sex and awaits me (the operator)."

Martin and Cynthia's commuter marriage faces such a deadlock. Cynthia has an excellent job as a teacher in the town where they lived for a number of years. Eighteen months ago Martin found a good job nearly 150 miles away. They agreed that he would live five days in High-Tech City, and she would hold down the fort in Welcome Home Village. They would spend the weekends together, and Martin would use vacation days to plan as many three- and four-day weekends as possible. It is a long drive to Welcome Home Village, and by the time Martin hits the driveway he thinks all sexual barriers had better be cleared. There had better not be any sexual gridlocks of competing family demands, and Cynthia's social calendar had best not create any sexual log-jams. After all, Martin's been away for a week, and he wants to start the weekend off right with Cynthia. He expects her to be instantly ready. Cynthia, too, has bought into the myth that their weekend and their marriage cannot succeed unless they experience instant Friday-night-sex success. They are headed for a deadlock once the glamor and the fatigue of instant up-to-speed sex wears off.

Serious problems occur when people buy into analogous thinking about desk top computers and apply it to marriage. There is no "delete" button or "erase" command in a marriage relationship regarding feelings, memories or attitudes. One can make an error on a computer and easily correct it. In human life an error never goes away. It is incorporated into the person's experience and into the relationship. Mistakes in sexual judgment and sensitivity occur just like errors in financial decisions or car purchases, with one exception: sexual decisions are far more critical for the survival of the marriage. It is dangerous to buy into a popular mythology of thinking your sexual partner is an object to be used.

A Right to Sex

A similar idea in Christian homes is that the husband has the unlimited right to demand sex. Betty is a true believer and has entered into a second marriage. From the beginning it has been a stormy relationship. During a long interval between the end of her first marriage and her new marriage, she and her new husband, Peter, had an extended courtship. Betty and Peter had been divorced for several years and were very lonely before their marriage. Therefore, sex had been an immediate attraction for them. Shortly after the marriage and long before the honeymoon period ended, Peter began to make more and more sexual demands of Betty. Sheepishly she admits that she likes sex any time of day. But it is not an all-consuming drive for her. Achieving love, intimacy, tenderness and joy in her life cannot be measured by the frequency of sexual intercourse. Peter protests that if they had sex as frequently as he wants, he would be totally responsive to Betty in other areas of life.

This couple's problem is not the frequency or the intensity of sexual intercourse. Their deadlock is a spiritual problem: as a Christian, Peter believes he's free to make sexual demands of his wife. Certainly both had a long period of sexual abstinence, and marriage is the place for sexual fulfillment. But *demanding* sexual intercourse, rather than inviting sexual intimacy, is not the way for Peter to honor Betty. Peter is stubborn in clinging to a popular myth that the husband must have sexual needs met first; then and only then will he submit to his wife's desire for closeness, hand-holding and gentleness.

There are other people who believe that sex is like a nightcap—the perfect ending to a day. The problem with this attitude is the selfishness in thinking that, "I am not satisfied, self-fulfilled or able to relax at night until I have sex." It's almost like going through sign-off procedures on a computer. You have to follow a certain shutdown sequence for the day's work to count. But trouble occurs when one focuses on one's own sexual needs without regard for the partner. Good sex in marriage should enhance the self-fulfillment of the *other*. It is not determined by one's need for a sexual nightcap.

A mythology that pervades our so-called post-Victorian culture is that all people want to have and should have sex frequently, intensely and with complete satisfaction. After all, we're no longer Puritans or prudes. It is the new sexual age, and we have enlightened ideas and a commitment to sexuality. But the mythology is just that. It does not approximate either Christian truth or the everyday experience of many. Fallacies of "liberated sex" impinge upon the Christian marriage, threatening to push it into marital deadlock. For example, in the mid-seventies Marabel Morgan proposed creating a sexual myth for Christian women, "The Total Woman." Morgan played on sexually explicit themes but disguised them with sexual cuteness. The message of her popular myth to Christian women was very direct: the more enticing, sexy and stimulating you can be to the man in your life, the better his sex life will be. But even more important, your marriage will then give you what you want. "Getting what you want," in the Morgan myth, means a new refrigerator or a mink coat rather than mutual satisfaction, intimacy and understanding.

The National Average

Many couples that I talk with are initially embarrassed to state they have sexual intercourse less frequently than the national norm. They believe that most couples, statistically speaking, have sex at least three, if not five, times a week.

Frequently a marriage partner or a couple may become frustrated that their sexual behavior is not always as exciting as they expected it to be. In a era of fast foods and instant meals, the popular myth that sex must be microwave-fast and thoroughly done is a powerful force. However, one partner's excitability rhythm may be slightly out-of-sync with the other's. One may be slower to arouse than the other, or one may have a low threshold for sexual excitement.

These differences in sexual rhythm can easily translate into impatience with the other partner. Women often learn to fake excitement in order to cope with their husband's impatience. Among older men, faking excitement becomes a challenge, especially if the wife is considerably younger. In both instances, the need to fake sexual satisfaction is based upon the myth that marriage must always be sexy.

Showing more enthusiasm than one feels is *faking* because it leads a sex partner to believe that one is completely satisfied when one isn't. Not wanting, liking or enjoying sex at all and pretending both interest and excitement is *deception*. Faking can slide into deception; deception will slip into resentment and bitterness. That often is followed by refusal to engage even in foreplay because it will lead to predictable, painful results.

Impatience regarding sex leads to a problematic playing out of the myth that marriage must always be sexy and sexual relations must always lead to orgasm.

It's a simple physiological fact for both men and women that orgasm does not always happen. Unless that fact is accepted, a husband or wife may feel like a failure, or wallow in the disappointment that "I cannot always make my partner have orgasm." An equally devastating response is, "There must be something wrong with me because I don't have orgasm every time I have sex." The truth is that sexual intercourse does not guarantee orgasm. Equally true is the fact that intercourse can be extremely satisfying without orgasm. To believe differently is to accept into the myth that good marriages produce good sex, and good sex produces orgasm one hundred percent of the time.

I Can Be Passive

Another problem which stems from the myth that marriage must be sexy is the feeling that one has the right to be sexually passive. In my book *Sex With Confidence* there is a chapter entitled "Are You Trapped in a Sexual Service Station?" In the chapter I discuss some of the manipulative joys of being sexually passive. In brief, the dilemma arises over the popular perception that if a person is a high producer in other areas of life, provides well for the family and is actively involved in church or civic affairs, he or she will be rewarded with a marriage partner who will always recharge the sexual batteries.

Jewel and Charles have been married for three stormy years. Both are dedicated Christians. She works hard in her small but successful domestic cleaning business. Charles has a highly demanding job as an air traffic controller. They have no children. As they describe it, some days they engage in a literal race to the house to determine who will be waited on sexually first. The myth behind these sexual demands is plain. The you-must-satisfy-me theme assumes, "Since I feel tired and deserve a reward for the labors and pressure of my workday, at night it is my turn to be sexually passive. You must make the marriage sexy for me."

Satisfying sex is a matter of mutuality and not a foot race to dive naked under the covers first and then dare the partner to "turn me on."

A variation on the high-tech sex myth is seen in the folks who stock up on sex manuals and video tapes. They always have an open ear to friends' gossip and to the latest exciting sexual technique. The partners develop a predetermined "specification list" about how the other must perform to make his or her sexual life satisfying.

The notion that one will lay back passively while the other performs to specifications on a sexual score card is self-defeating. This attitude takes the popular myth of marriage being sexy and exploits the half that says, "It must always be sexy for me." This is based upon a sex "spec sheet" that is torn from porn. It is not a page from the mutuality advocated by Scripture. Rather its origin is hearsay, graphs, drawings and videos of other folks in very different, generally unloving circumstances.

In this kind of battlefield, the conflict focuses on frustrations of premature ejaculation and impotence. For instance, Monica and Harold have been married for a number of years. He has always had a chronic complaint which for years he voiced only to himself: "My wife is not as sexually exciting and stimulating as I want her to be." Captured by the boldness of the popular myth that his life deserves to be more sexy, Harold has challenged Monica to be more sexy. Surprisingly, at least to Harold, she picked up his gauntlet. Now she's more of a sexual dynamo than he had anticipated and, to make matters worse for him, her newly discovered sexual energy is causing him to have premature ejaculation. What a blow this is to his male ego. The bedroom has become an embarrassing battle zone. This does not fit his script. His wife was supposed to be a Marilyn Monroe figure who turned him on. But with her sexual energy and joy, Monica teasingly presses her bedroom advantage. Life has become too sexy for Harold; he simply cannot control himself, and Monica loves it!

Doug and Nancy have also been married for some time and have two college-aged children. Doug, like Harold, chides his wife to be more sexually responsive. Doug works hard, is successful and thinks all Nancy has to do is manage the household and get ready for his arrival in the bedroom. We see some of Marybelle Morgan's influence in Doug's fantasies about Nancy's sexiness. But now the tables are turned. Uncertain about its source but absolutely devastated by its consequence, Doug is discovering his impotence. He can't perform according to his specifications. Can he scale down his sexy life? Will Nancy press the advantage of her newfound sexual potency? Certainly this is emotional fodder for a soap opera. In the meantime, Doug's impotency flattens his notion that because he is a high-level producer, he can be sexually passive in the bedroom. He did not bargain to be so passive that he is impotent! In both Harold's and Doug's cases the response to the myth that "I don't get sex" has run amok.

Excessive Sensitivity

Sam and Denise have a different problem. Married for nearly four years, they enjoy sex and are faithful to one another. But now, with a one-year-old son and increased career responsibilities, their sexual life has taken a sudden and frustrating down-turn.

Their dilemma is not the direct sexual passivity noted in the case of Jewel and Charles. Because they love each other, they have become sensitive about not wanting to "force" the other in sexual matters. They understand all the problems of faking sexual satisfaction—sexual cuteness, impatience and the fact that orgasm is not automatic. Their deadlock is in not wanting to create a sense of sexual obligation for the other. This ties them into an emotional gridlock of not taking sexual initiative if there is no clear sign, indication or hint the other partner is ready. This couple's deadlock is an over-sensitive reaction against the popular myth that marriage must be sexy.

If marriage is going to be appropriately sexy, adequate and sophisticated, foreplay is the secret to the success. Good foreplay occurs long before one reaches an impassioned embrace. It may begin with a mid-day phone call or an invitation to dinner or the luxury of a gentle evening walk. The possibilities are limitless. The more subtle and gradual the interplay of foreplay with social, conversational and even religious activities, the greater the likelihood the marriage will be genuinely sexy.

We are not sexual computers or nudity specialists. Marriage and sexual intercourse can be sexy and delightful when couples move beyond the notion that high-tech sex and special-effects techniques guarantee sexual satisfaction.

Perhaps the most difficult myth to overcome is the self-deception found in the attitude that one spouse can be sexually passive, and the other must turn him or her. This attitude is encapsulated in the foolish statement, "Marriage must be sexy on my terms."

Christian Truth:
We Do Not Live by Sex Alone

Without sexual procreation, each generation is the last frontier of civilization. The Scriptures clearly inform us that we are to marry, be fruitful and multiply. Sex and sexuality are part of God's plan for creation and for us as human beings and members of God's creation.

Our call, surely, is to be sexual beings. But our sexuality is not to become such an obsession that we confuse marriage, sexuality and being human with living by sex alone.

Sex is definitely a part of who we are as human beings, and yet in Genesis we are told, "The Lord God formed man from the dust of the ground and breathed into his nostrils the breath of life, and man became a living being" (Genesis 2:7). The "breath of life" distinguishes us from other creatures. The breath of life is our spiritual nature, and it gives us communion and covenant with God. So sex is satisfying, but it is not the entirety of what inspires us as human beings.

The Affair

Affairs seem to be quite a status symbol these days. Whether people are Christians or not, the word on the street is that the mid-life crisis of a male or female is always associated with an affair. Of course, popular sex myths shroud mid-life crises too. When one examines affairs, one quickly recognizes far deeper needs than "a last fling," "taking care of my sexual needs" or "rediscovering my sexual potency with a younger partner."

The real issue is not one of pure animalistic potency. Rather, the root problems stem from control, intimacy, loneliness, abandonment, fear of success and fear of failure. But in ninety percent of the cases with which I am familiar, "pure sex" is not the source of the marital deadlock.

When people reflect on how they get into an affair, they point to aspects of foreplay far more subtle than direct sexual or physical contact. Often it comes as a word of affirmation, an inviting sense of humor, a gentle "good morning" at work, a reassuring smile in the face of disappointment, a willingness to listen, accept and understand. None of these activities are in and of themselves likely to make a free-association checklist of sexual activities. But often they are the ignition point for an affair. They are so powerful and seductive because they form a bridge between explicit sexual behavior and the pure, warm milk of human kindness.

If a spouse finds a mate involved in an affair, the most effective and least painful way of breaking it up and reasserting the integrity of the relationship is to begin some positive emotional bridge-building. If you can do that, then the fruit of the Spirit will bless the relationship. More often than not the person with whom the spouse is having an affair is not sexually attractive by comparative standards to the spouse. The real purpose of most affairs is not sexual intercourse alone. Rather it is an effort to discover or rediscover deeper aspects of the breath of life. As Christians we have the inside track on how to receive and enhance the breath of life in ourselves and our marriage partners.

Financial conflicts, parent-child relationships, job disappointments and other wedlock deadlocks are translated into good excuses for hiding behind sexual affairs. For the Christian, a partner's affair is both spiritually and emotionally painful, embarrassing and devastating of marital trust. People are reluctant to turn to their pastors in such circumstances because the affair seems to be the unpardonable sin. A couple will fear talking to trusted friends at church or at work because it starts gossip. Friends may laugh. Often the feelings of betrayal, disbelief and depression immobilize both partners.

The partner wronged by the active affair of the spouse often fails to obtain help when it's most needed. The problem is further exacerbated and the marriage frequently driven into despair because both husband and wife identify strictly and solely with the sexual dimension of the illicit relationship.

Just an Excuse

However, the first principle to remember is that the affair is often just an excuse for coping with other problems in the marriage. We need to remember that sex is important, but it can't be *that* important. Therefore when people find themselves or their partners involved in affairs, more often than not sex is not the driving force behind it. The problem is also more devastating and more complex than the spiritual legalism of whether or not someone has committed adultery.

In the same way that the affair is a good excuse for avoiding or failing to cope with other non-sexual pressures in the marriage, marriage partners must be careful not to hide in their sexuality. The spiritual, emotional and marital fallacy behind the Marabel Morgan program is that one is encouraged to hide behind sexual behavior. If one can be sexually cute and seductive, if sexual behavior seems satisfying, if sex is frequent and orgasm always present, the conclusion seems obvious: everything is right in heaven and on earth. We should know better. We do not live by sex alone.

In a culture filled with high-tech "overkill" we must constantly be vigilant to return to a simple way of life. We live with too many excesses, only a few of which are directly sexual. The excessive use of automotive horsepower, reconstructive surgery, aerobics, self-help books and spiritual retreats does not lead to simplicity.

Sexual excess, therefore, is born of the spirit of the times. If we can rid ourselves of excesses, the power of the popular myth that marriage must always be sexy will resolve itself into a proper perspective. We are confronting the principalities and powers of an age that dwells on over-stimulation. Being over-stimulated is not satisfying, it's frustrating. Sex satisfies—but only in the context of gentle, sensitive, extended foreplay and the context of a life of balanced activities and relationships. Over-stimulation is the arch enemy of satisfactory sex.

At the periphery of sexual behavior, the subtle differences between foreplay and pseudo-sexual teasing are difficult to discern.

Consider the case of Wilbur and Heidi. She is a very attractive, seductive individual. Wilbur is a "salt-of-the-earth" man who prides himself in being married to an attractive and sexy woman. Across the years they both have had difficulty in understanding the mixed sexual messages Heidi sends. When she's depressed it's hard for her to believe she is genuinely attractive and sexually alluring. When she's sexually turned on she uses her charm, wit and sensuality in overpowering ways. It is difficult for Wilbur, as well as for males at work, to distinguish between a true come-on and just being friendly. Heidi is totally dedicated to being faithful in her marriage. She winds up, however, giving mixed and false messages to other males.

Heidi's marriage, her sexuality and her capacity to engage in true intimacy will increase as she learns to give clearer, more consistent messages. One can be appropriately intimate at work, enjoying people, being charming and even a bit flirtatious with those who understand that she's not offering a "come on." This behavior is merely an extension of who she is and provides a context within which appropriate social intimacy is realized. At the same time Heidi must learn not to be quite as flirtatious or charming until she and her male colleagues are able to distinguish better what is simply an outgoing and gregarious behavior from teasing foreplay.

In Heidi's family background one can sense a history of very little social intimacy between parents and children. Heidi scarcely remembers any sexual intimacy between her father and mother. She did not have good role models for intimacy in her youth. During her teenage and young adult years, Heidi experienced a lot of sexual pain, some of which happened because she had not experienced true intimacy. When discouraged, Heidi fears any intimacy because she remembers all too quickly the pain associated with youthful efforts at closeness. At the same time she wants closeness and intimacy through her spirituality, social activities and human relationships. But Heidi has to move beyond her pain. As she learns to trust others not to translate interpersonal warmth into direct foreplay, the pain of not knowing true intimacy will begin to dissipate, and Heidi will begin to discover for herself and her husband the reality of not living by sex alone.

If we are going to put aside the popular myth that marriage always has to be sexy and that life without sex is intolerable, then we must understand that true intimacy is not a euphemism for sexual intercourse. True intimacy involves sexual components because to be human is to be sexual.

The Breath of Life

The breath of life that characterizes us as human beings is the unique gift that God gives, and it points toward the discovery of true intimacy. God's breath of life invites us to be spiritually, emotionally and even physically vulnerable to one another. Intimacy of spirit is the most profound expression of closeness that we can achieve. At the same time we must not spiritualize intimacy so as to endorse an equally misleading popular spiritual myth that spirituality excludes sexuality.

The vulnerability of true intimacy calls us not to hide, mask or stifle the breath of life offered us by God and the spiritual scent we may offer another. Vulnerability in the pew, the work place, the kitchen, the living room and the bedroom invites us to discover a full measure of true human intimacy. Sex is important, but it is only one component of true intimacy.

In Sum

Intimacy is more than sexual intercourse. If marriages are to be fun, they do need to be sexy. Popular mythology limits sexiness to explicit sexual behavior, however. That's a misleading understanding of sex, intimacy and marriage and provides a license for affairs, withdrawal, impotence and sexual violence.

The Christian truth affirms the important and essential role of sex in human life, especially in marriage where sexual intercourse is a culminating gesture of physical intimacy. But we are more than sexual intercourse. We are more than our explicit sexual behavior.

The breath of life given to human beings by God in the act of creation invites us to participate in the fullness of our sexual behavior. This uniquely spiritual dimension of human life is God-given and joins us to the principle that we do not live by sex alone. Interpersonal relations, family relations and our relationship with God blend with our sexuality to provide a unity of experience that, with God's help, enables us to live life to its fullest with God, with friends and with our bodies.

Four

Do You Like It? Charge It!

Popular Myth:
Enjoy Yourself Now! Somebody Else Will Pay for It

Christian Truth:
Store Up for Yourselves Treasures in Heaven

Popular Myth:
Enjoy Yourself Now! Somebody Else Will Pay for It

Another way of stating this popular myth is, "Someone else will take care of me." The challenge of this myth is especially threatening to Christians because it sounds so much like "living by faith," trusting that God will take care of you in all circumstances. But adopting this myth leads to deadlock when people find themselves in serious trouble because they didn't plan for the future or take responsibility for their behavior. Aaron and Pam are an example of a couple who found themselves in financial difficulties after buying into this myth. When I first talked with them, Aaron practically shoved Pam into my office. We were meeting at his request, and the reason quickly became obvious. I observed that Aaron was highly perfectionistic and cradled his amateur's delight in his financial investment skills. He was angry because his wife couldn't seem to control her charge card spending. Aaron's words were, "Pam is in deep plastic." She had ignored her charge card bills for months and then refinanced them, agreeing to "loan shark" interest rates of nearly twenty-six percent interest. Both husband and wife were deeply embarrassed.

Aaron was sure his wife was totally out of control; Pam agreed she was but pleaded that her husband was unsympathetic.

Aaron had attended a Christian money management seminar and was committed to a "cash only" approach to all family finances. He conceded a monthly car payment, but he paid all his personal expenses with cash. Still, it was clear that part of Pam's overspending stemmed from the fact that Aaron had talked her into buying his professional gifts and paying for their entertainment expenses. Her modest income as an executive secretary in a local computer service company would not support household expenses and their entertainment costs. Aaron, nonetheless, saw her as out of control. Pam claimed that he was unrealistic in how thin her money could be spread.

Looking at the facts and figures, it became clear that while Pam gives in to impulse-spending, Aaron yields to denial. He would not admit that their household activities were so expensive and that Pam could not reasonably cover the expenses assigned to her without falling deeper into debt. The plastic had really hit the financial fan: Her impulsiveness! His perfectionism!

Buying the Kids' Affection

Pam and Aaron's problem is put in perspective by another case. Valerie was furious at Luke because he couldn't control his spending habits. Luke was on the road a great deal and missed closeness and companionship with his two pre-adolescent sons. He showered time, lavish gifts, money and patience on the boys to maintain his warm relationship with them.

As we discussed the problem, Luke admitted that some of his excessive gift-giving came from insecurity that his wife would grow closer to his sons than he, and he wanted to remind his boys how much he loved them. The second part of the problem centered on the boys' perception of Luke's insecurity. At times they played him for all they could get. That left Valerie in the middle—furious, hurt, insecure—and Beth, the daughter, completely out in the cold. Besides, Valerie was left with the household finances and knew better than anyone else that Luke was unable to control his spending habits.

Both cases illustrate an "If you like it, charge it!" mentality. The surface pleasure of spending is actually an effort to conquer a deeper insecurity and a sincere desire to please others.

Many Christian families struggle with being "in deep plastic." The challenge of Christian truth is for families to move out of deep plastic, out of the shallow shoals of impulsive buying, to move more freely in the deeper waters of mutual respect and responsibility.

Someone Will Bail Me Out

Sometimes people depend on others, not just their credit cards, to save them. Fran is a gentle-spirited "will-o-the-wisp." Her husband, Gary, is also a free spirit. When Fran becomes anxious about life, she talks about escaping with her husband to some mystical, spiritual abode where life is uncomplicated and will always work out well for them. In the real world of job opportunities, rent obligations and a commitment to peace and justice, she flies into financial brick walls on the wings of her spiritual romanticism. Fran and Gary believe what only a few people dare say, "Jesus, or somebody else, will always take care of me." She acts daily on that belief, often by carrying very little money and no calendar. Fran survives on her intuitive enthusiasm, imaginative maneuvering and Gary's laid-backness as she moves from one crisis to the next.

One day, as she was discussing some of her problems with Annette, a close girlfriend, she suddenly remembered she had to rush home to prepare a meal. Fran reddened as she realized that she didn't have a car. The state inspection sticker had run out three months previously, and on that day the local police, unsurprised by her absentmindedness, had reminded her gently that she could not drive her vehicle minus the sticker. Now the car was parked at her favorite gas station waiting inspection.

Gary couldn't be reached, so she called a taxi. Annette walked with her to curbside to await the cab. After a typical rush-hour traffic delay of several minutes, the cabbie arrived, quickly picked up his fare and bolted on his way. Less than fifty yards from the pick-up point, the cab screeched to a halt! Fran leaped out of the car and ran back toward Annette—Fran had no cash for the taxi ride home! Annette didn't have much cash either, but she dug deep into her belongings and came up with $5.45. She didn't think it would be enough to get Fran home, but it was all she had.

The next day, Fran called Annette to express her gratitude and to assure her that she arrived home safely. She said she would mail Annette a check for $5.45, but asked her not to cash it for a week until she or Gary could get some money into her "crazy" checking account.

Fran could not face the reality that cars require state safety inspections, cab drivers expect to be paid and friends are not petty cash boxes. Fran is like many people who claim to depend upon Jesus, the pastor, husband, wife or friends to always bail them out. It's a lot easier than planning ahead with personal finances.

Fran owes it to herself, to Jesus, to her family, to co-workers and to Annette to think ahead. If she would, Fran wouldn't have to feel so guilty about running out of money, and other people wouldn't have to be so anxious about always having to bail her out. The love could be more genuine and pure between Fran and her friends and probably between Fran and Gary if she would think of the future.

Major League Ambitions

Jack has a similar inability to face financial reality. He and Sharon have been married for eight years and have a two-year-old daughter they adore. They also have budget planning problems. Sharon has a good job as a sales representative for a national computer firm, loves her work, pulls down a good salary and is unfailing in her commitment to the marriage. Jack is a gifted athlete. He was a baseball star in college and spent a couple of years in the semi-pros before they married. Jack is a kind of Crash Davis figure from the movie *Bull Durham,* the bright but perpetual minor-leaguer. A good-looking, affable, highly intelligent and morally straight individual, Jack has managed to endear himself to many people. Every kid who shows good athletic promise entertains some fantasy of being in the pros, landing a big salary and frolicking in an opulent lifestyle. Many people who have money but few athletic skills surround themselves with athletes in order to enhance their self-images. Some of Jack's nonathletic but financially successful friends had recruited him to work for them in a national sales networking organization. All the symbols of financial success were dangled daily in his face.

A decade later and now in his mid-thirties, Jack still chases after the big league bucks, but they are as elusive as were his big league dreams. Sharon actually provides most of the family's predictable and substantial income. Jack keeps talking big money but will not make a commitment to plan a budget or to state an actual dollar figure he will contribute to his family's welfare. This situation reminds one of Jesus' teaching about the wisdom of someone wanting to build a house. He said to count the cost before beginning construction. An important principle of sound fiscal planning for the Christian is to count the cost. While Jack is wrapped up in the popular myth, "Do you like it? Charge it!", he is not literally using a charge card. He *is* displaying a "charge it to my wife" attitude. If this marriage is going to grow, both Sharon and Jack must commit themselves to being financially responsible.

Slipping into deep plastic and believing that someone else will bail us out when we act irresponsibly are serious outgrowths of the "Do you like it? Charge it!" myth. Another problem related to this myth revolves around the inability to control impulsive behavior. One reason for such impulsive spending is immaturity.

Fiscal Immaturity

Wayne comes from a Christian family. His father has been permanently hospitalized in a Veteran's Administration hospital because of injuries sustained in Vietnam. His mother is a hardworking school teacher, frugal almost to a fault. Wayne, however, has been through a college education, one wife, numerous cars, nearly as many jobs and now is back home in his mother's house—against her better judgment. Unwilling to accept the responsibility for his underachievement in college, his underemployment and his unwillingness to be a real husband to his former wife, he has a new game—blackmailing mother with threats of suicide. He says if she won't take out loans to help him play out his scenario, "Do you like it? Charge it!", he will kill himself.

Wayne has never moved beyond his immaturity of believing that his life is made of fast cars, fast women and fast bucks. His wife divorced him for the same reason his mother feels like divorcing him. He manipulates and blackmails to get someone else to pay for his impulses. Sooner or later Wayne's mother is going to have to call his blackmail bluff. She must stop dishing out the money, covering for him in his alimony obligations and lying to his employer when he doesn't show up for work and she has no idea of his whereabouts. Without taking that step of faith, Wayne's mother is simply reinforcing his immaturity and making it more difficult for him to gain control over his impulses. She will have to allow Wayne to suffer the consequences of his behavior, a lesson he should have learned before leaving home.

I Owe it to Me

Karen's immaturity reveals itself in another way. A moody only child, Karen has turned aside many opportunities for marriage. She complains about how life mistreats her, about her low income and about her parents' emotional and financial dependence. Karen is always broke, grimly smiling but continually complaining of some physical ailment.

As a child, she converted her negative mood swings into demanding that her parents give her money for ice cream, movies, clothes and trips. Now twenty-five years out of high school, still single and still living at home, her mood swings are just as strong, if not more accentuated. At times Karen leaves the impression that she wants to get herself into a bad mood so that she can say, "I owe myself something good!" This phase triggers permission to buy clothing and accessories. When she's mad at the world, she buys herself something.

Karen's guilt from not controlling her impulses is making her more difficult to live with. Karen needs to learn that she can love herself without getting angry as an excuse for doing something good for herself. Life could be much more cheerful and the possibility of being happily married could also be a greater possibility. But first she has to put something in the center of her life beyond the "I owe me" attitude.

Addictive Spending

Another, perhaps more destructive, aspect of the "Do you like it? Charge it!" syndrome is addictive spending. Like other addictive behaviors, the temptation to spend, spend, spend never goes away. Many people dismiss the thought of demons as immature and ridiculous. However, a close examination of the literature on addictive behavior, whether relating to drugs, alcohol, gambling, spending, eating or sex, reveals that it is a form of demon possession. It will not go away through good thoughts or natural maturation. Special efforts must be made to break the addiction.

Gloria, for example, is married to Matthew, a highly successful investment broker. During the entirety of their fifteen year marriage, they have enjoyed an affluent lifestyle, and there's nothing to indicate they will not continue to be financially blessed. Because he's an investment broker, Matthew gives a great deal of time and attention to budget planning and has allocated an excessive amount to Gloria for clothing. Their entertainment needs rose automatically with Matthew's income, and he initially saw no problem with Gloria's lavish outfits. However, a closer look at her spending patterns reveals a compulsion to buy more and more clothing that she wears less and less. Following a heart-to-heart discussion, Matthew and Gloria agreed she would cut down on her spending patterns. However, one day Matthew came home from work and opened the trunk of their car to pick up a can of tennis balls. He was stunned to discover nearly $1,000 worth of clothing hidden beneath several empty shopping bags.

Gloria's addiction to self-indulgent spending stems from an insecure family background, coupled with a deep belief that anybody or anything may not be there for her tomorrow. She's certain she will inevitably be rejected. Therefore, she hordes clothes as though she were a squirrel storing nuts for the winter hibernation.

Gloria has a serious problem. She's gone beyond simple buying sprees to the financial addiction "Do you like it? Charge it!" She buys to feel secure, but her self-indulgence fails to make her enjoy life.

Over-Spenders Anonymous

For years Alcoholics Anonymous (AA) has had a definite ministry to those afflicted with alcoholism. In recent years, variations on AA's theme have been applied to compulsive gambling, eating and sex. Clearly there is a need for an organization such as Over Spenders Anonymous.

The common thread in all these organizations is that an individual cannot save himself or herself. No amount of positive thoughts, remorse, guilt or understanding of the problem will change the fact that the behavior is beyond self-control. In eleven of the twelve steps in their "Program for Recovery," A.A. declares that the spiritual dimension is absolutely essential for permanent change.

To sum it up, the popular myth of "Do you like it? Charge it!" reflects the false belief that a "Big Daddy," represented by Jesus, a spouse or the end of the world, will solve one's problems. Some leap at the state lottery or a perfect lover to make their lives complete. However, nowhere in Scripture are we taught to sit passively, waiting for God or others to do something magical for us. The dangerous myth that promotes the philosophy of "Enjoy it now, somebody else will pay for it later" is the devil's happy hunting ground.

Those who recognize that they're entrapped in addictive behaviors begin their restoration and recovery with the frank admission that "the beast is always within me, ready to take charge." Only those who acknowledge they are not able to control themselves and need help are in a position to drive the demons into outer darkness.

Christian Truth:
Store Up for Yourselves Treasures in Heaven

To begin to apply this Christian truth to their lives, couples and individuals must face the reality that there are no magical bail outs and that, as Christians, we must be concerned with the eternal results of our behavior.

Jack and Sharon realize this now and are trying to get their budget under control. Their success will not only be measured with numbers, but it will also come as Jack makes a realistic assessment of the cost of building his marriage. He dare not worry about those who have made it financially in sports or investments.

A sure sign that Jack and Sharon are on their way to fiscal responsibility occurred when Jack was willing to commit to a two-fold program. Jack agreed to meet with Sharon and carve out a realistic budget that reduces all the talk to dollars and cents, even if the family must make some sacrifices. As the second component, and to prevent Jack from becoming bogged down in the minutia of daily financial details, I asked that he and Sharon plan a financially responsible seven-day vacation for themselves sometime in the next two years. By committing themselves to save for a vacation, Sharon and Jack were able to avoid some of their impulsive, unsatisfying and expensive last-minute vacations. The rationale for planning a good, even exotic, vacation is to break impulsive activities and to plan ahead.

No More Plastic

Fran is also experiencing some victory over her financial entanglements. Shortly after borrowing the $5.45 from Annette for cab fare, she dropped by her pastor's office and told her the story. With a smile she reached into her handbag, pulled out two plastic credit cards and handed them to her. "I can live without plastic!" Fran declared victoriously. "You keep these for me. In case of a genuine emergency, I want to check with you before I use them. Right now I don't ever want to see them again!"

Jack, Sharon and Fran, all Christians, are beginning to store up for themselves spiritual treasures in heaven. The teaching of Jesus has less to do with fiscal management than with personal life management. Treasures in heaven refer to one's ultimate and primary allegiance. Poor planning, addictive spending or unrealistic expectations that someone else will always bail you out can be put aside. These people are learning that there is no magical bail-out. Credit problems do not go away, and one doesn't get to start over. Learning to plan a vacation two years in advance and being able to live without credit cards are forms of laying up for yourself treasures in heaven.

In Matthew 25, Jesus told a parable of the ten virgins. He considered five wise and five foolish. The foolish virgins sat, waiting for someone else to take care of them. The wise virgins, who were prepared for the bridegroom and eventually entered the wedding feast, did two major things Jesus also expects of us.

Plan Ahead

Most couples, married or about to marry, resist talking about and establishing a budget. Budget planning involves more than dollars and cents. It involves personal values. People claim living within a budget depersonalizes the family and reduces it to nothing more than a business transaction. However, *budget planning is value planning.* For instance, your values reflect how you spend your money. One person may acquire books, another new clothes, still another photographic equipment. One family might prefer to spend extra dollars on a swimming pool for the back yard; another might choose a trip to Disney World. We do not live in a value-free society, and we dare not attempt a value-free marriage.

The wise virgins also planned ahead and budgeted their oil and their time. A financial plan lays up for the marriage a treasure that cannot be measured in dollars. It can give the family something to look forward to, protect it from the stress of too many monthly payments or offer security in case of emergencies.

Another component of being a fiscally wise virgin is making certain that recreational opportunities are available for the family. This does not mean the husband does what he wants, the wife has her plans and the children have still other activities. Recreation is important. The old adage, "All work and no play makes Jack a dull boy," is still true. Fun times must be done as a family. But this takes wise financial planning.

Do Little Things Along the Way

Couples who do not plan ahead become near-sighted in their commitments to each other, to their recreational needs and to their budget planning. Of course there's always a danger in plans becoming grandiose. The secret to success is to behave as the wise virgins. Keep your budget and financial dreams simple. Keep them under control. And be prepared to act. Carry an extra supply of oil (a savings account), keep the wicks trimmed with gentle pruning of intention (carefully think through the plans) and be poised to go into the feast (any situation in life) with readiness to seize a good opportunity.

Treasures in Heaven

It's one thing to be wise, but how does one store up treasures in heaven? One way is to develop *quiet time*, a personal time with God. Our daily quiet times are like a mini-Sabbath. We need to reflect continuously on the meaning of life, the direction of our lives, the opportunities for tomorrow, our values and our resources. This spiritual envisagement can only be accomplished in quiet and relaxed times. The wise virgins went quietly about their business, but they did the little things along the way that counted.

The foolish virgins were content to wait for someone else to take initiative instead of cultivating their own relationships with God. There's nothing immoral about not lugging along a backpack of oil, a pair of scissors and new wicks. The wise virgins, however, packed up extra oil and trimming devices and were alert when the feast began. The biggest and most dangerous temptations come through inactivity and passivity.

Therein lies the difference between the wise and the foolish virgins. The wise virgins planned ahead and did the little things along the way to make certain they would arrive prepared at their final destination.

As a disciple, Peter displayed immature, impulsive, self-indulgent, insecure and insensitive behavior. But at Pentecost, which followed his seashore encounter with Jesus, Peter was imbued with new power and miraculously became head of the Jerusalem church. In Peter's life we see three clues to marital deadlocks over immature, impulsive and addictive behaviors.

1. Learn Self-control

The secret to self-control is not self-determination. It is the confession that one has a need and must have another's help. The success of Alcoholics Anonymous is the willingness of each member to commit to allowing other people to help. One is expected to attend weekly, sometimes daily, meetings whether there is a *felt* need or not. Each must continue to confess both neediness and progress made.

Learning self-control requires inviting other people to help break personal deadlocks with impulsive and immature behavior. This is the deathgrip of impulsive behavior. Peter had to learn self-control by becoming more dependent upon others, including Jesus and his fellow disciples. At Pentecost Peter began to trust the Holy Spirit. The community of faith that miraculously emerged from the confusion, anxiety and spiritual uncertainty allowed the church to minister to and through him. He no longer resorted to impulsive actions to conquer his fears. Peter had gained spiritual and personal self-control.

2. Care for Others

The power of Pentecost transformed Peter into a peacemaker. This breakthrough occurred in public with many people caring for one another. Too many Christian couples indulge their pipe dreams in splendid isolation. If you have a good idea about what you want to do with your life, don't keep it to yourself. Allow the Holy Spirit to establish a level of communication not previously realized. Share your dreams with your spouse. Plan together for the future. Care enough to invite your spouse to share his or her dreams with you. The secret of the New Testament church and Peter's leadership was in their learning to care for one another. It made the New Testament church come alive. And it will make a marriage work.

3. Nurture One Another

Provide for today's needs. The impulsive spender believes "charging it," while quickly looking the other way, will take care of things. Recall Gloria, who hid $1,000 worth of clothes in her car trunk; Karen, who always owes herself new clothes when angry or depressed; and Wayne, who blackmails his mother with suicide threats. The day's real needs are not met by impulsive purchases. They are best met as we learn to nuture one another.

As we are told in Acts, John Mark was rejected by the apostle Paul on their first missionary trip and sent back to Jerusalem for more training. Peter, the peacemaker, had the responsibility to nurture John Mark, his mother and the Jerusalem church, leading them to care for one another. Like the lilies of the field, Peter learned through nurturing not to worry so much about tomorrow's needs. Instead he was willing to meet others' needs that day.

Many people who end up in financially irresponsible behavior are desperately trying to ward off insecurity, fear and rejection. The things they buy are substitutes for being nurtured. At Pentecost, Peter began putting aside his impulsive and immature behavior. As he came to care for others, they learned to care for him. The reciprocal caring became a mutual transformation. The impulsive and out-of-control behavior began to fade into the past.

Hope for the Future

There is no sure cure for the addiction "Do you like it? Charge it!" But there is hope.

Like the process of sanctification that leads ever toward completeness in this life, we must continually be vigilant over lack of planning, impulse control failure and addictive spending. In Matthew 18:4, Jesus says, "Whoever humbles himself like this child is the greatest in the kingdom of heaven." What is the hallmark of the little child? Certainly, it is *not* independence. Little children are quick to declare neediness: "I need a drink." "My toe hurts." "I'm sick." "Johnny hates me." "Susie's always picking on me." Little children are like Jesus who in John 4 approached the Samaritan woman by Jacob's well, declaring his need for a drink.

If left to ourselves we never succeed in overcoming the temptation to be over-spenders, impulsive doers, immature actors and self-destructive ritualists. The first and most important step in change is to admit a perpetual neediness and to acknowledge that we will never be over sin or the charge card syndrome. At best we are "recovering alcoholics" or "recovering plasticholics," sinners on the way to maturity.

Acknowledging that one's deadlock with addictive spending is always in process is a first step. Appropriating the truth of putting on the mind of Christ is essential. But what does it mean to put on the mind of Christ? I believe there are three important steps.

1. Humility

In Philippians 2:6-8, we are told that Christ did not grasp after his equality with God, but rather he emptied himself of that status, independence and power. Jesus took on human form and the role of a servant. In so doing, he humbled himself in order to invite us to be his followers. "The Son of Man did not come to be served" (Matthew 20:28). The first step in putting on the mind of Christ is humility.

2. Supplication

A. B. Simpson, the nineteenth-century Presbyterian revivalist, speaks of the two hands of God. The one humbles us. The second hand receives humble, intercessory prayers and pleas of supplication and lifts us up.* "Cast all your anxiety on him because he cares for you" (1 Peter 5:7). It is God through Christ who is the "two hands" that embrace us and give us the mind of Christ. Don't be afraid to praise and to plea.

3. Persistence

In 1 Timothy 6:12, Paul admonishes and encourages Timothy to fight the good fight of faith. Timothy is to take hold of eternal life. The call to persistence and the assurance of eternal life are both Timothy's and our calling. Paul offers Timothy affirmation that in so doing he makes the boldest profession of faith to all. Don't be afraid to be who you are. Paul's message admonishes us to take hold of the faith given to you; then your life and mind become the mind of Christ.

In Sum

In planning ahead and doing little things along the way to prepare for entering the marriage feast, we are challenged to become the wise virgins, ready to respond to the invitation for life. The unwise virgins were not those who were involved in sexually promiscuous behavior. They were simply the women who

---

*A. B. Simpson, *Days of Heaven on Earth* (Camp Hill, Penn.: Christian Publications, 1984), May 26 selection. Originally published in 1897.

slipped into a deadlock due to neglect. When the decisive moment came, they wanted to "charge it." But the feast was for those who had moved beyond that deadlock.

Impulsive and addictive spending is the devil's calling card. It never goes away on its own. One must be vigilant and dare not relax, lest the demons and the beasts overwhelm and overpower. We must keep our lives in spiritual perspective, knowing there are some deadlocks we cannot overcome by ourselves. However as Peter found out, there are others willing and able to help us if we will let them. But the first important step in breaking the deadlock of the over-spender's syndrome of "Do you like it? Charge it!" is acknowledging our neediness *and* working through the problem with family and friends guided by Christian truths.

Five

I'm Getting an Attorney

Popular Myth:
My Marriage Needs a Quick Fix

Christian Truth:
The Law Destroys; the Spirit Builds

Popular Myth: My Marriage Needs a Quick Fix

The curse upon many marriages is the popular myth that states: "If I don't get my way, I'll fix you. I'll get my attorney—I'll sue!" When that attitude is allowed to creep into the inner life of a marriage, the results are disastrous. The invitation of the gospel is true for a marriage as well as for salvation: the power of the law can destroy a relationship. The Christian truth needed to guide one's marriage is the principle that the Spirit builds, and couples must rid themselves of the vindictive and libelous spirit of legalism.

Amazingly, this attitude is prevalent among people with strong Christian backgrounds. Blair grew up in a family of Baptist ministers and missionaries. Her husband, Earl, comes from a family of active Methodists. In twelve years of marriage, Blair and Earl intellectually considered themselves Christians. Wherever they were, they made sure their children were involved in a church that had strong Sunday school and youth programs. Long-suffering and easy-going on the surface, Blair had come to tolerate Earl's verbal abuse that seemed directly related to tension on his job. An innocuous incident triggered Earl's temper one night. He did not strike Blair, but the ensuing argument terrified everyone, including Earl, who had thrown a couple of dishes against the kitchen walls, breaking them and making a mess.

That night, Blair kicked Earl out of the house. He found a small apartment and agreed to live there until the dust settled on their very serious wedlock deadlock. Blair was convinced she should file for a legal separation.

Beneath the surface, Blair and Earl love one another and their children deeply. While embarrassed, hurt and angry over the recurring fights, neither one wanted a divorce.

As they unloaded their heartaches and problems in their pastor's study, he observed beneath Blair's easy-going veneer an enslaving and self-defeating perfectionism. She has never been satisfied that she measured up to her family's high spiritual expectations of her, even in insignificant matters. Now when she feels threatened, her perfectionism kicks into high gear. When threatened by Earl's loss of temper, she becomes caught in her own sense of inadequacy and inability to please. Then she projects the perceived perfectionistic demands of others onto her husband, children and colleagues.

This is why, following the big fight, Blair decided Earl had to leave. Quick and decisive legal action formalizing their separation was necessary, she thought, to cope with her perfectionism and his temper.

Legal Wrongs, Moral Wrongs

When marital battles occur, as they inevitably will in the best of Christian marriages, two types of wrongs must be separated from each other: acts that may be legally wrong and acts that may be morally or spiritually wrong.

Buddy and Joyce are in deadlock because he has demanded absolute control of family finances. He believes this is his right as head of the household. This has caused conflict since Joyce's parents' estate settlement five years ago. The settlement involved direct payment of dividends to Joyce for use in their childrens' future educational needs.

But Buddy has not honored that settlement. He has been using the dividend monies to cover family operating expenses. This is a case of moral *and* legal wrong-doing. Buddy has misappropriated funds clearly designated by law for a specific purpose.

Remember Luke, who gives his sons lavish gifts when he returns from business trips to make up for the time spent away from them? He and his wife, Valerie, ran into problems when Luke borrowed from the children's education fund to pay for his gifts to them. Clearly he intends to pay back the money, and he feels a great deal of moral guilt. There is no legal requirement that Luke or Valerie save money for their children's education, and they have not legally restricted the money they've saved for that purpose. This is a moral commitment. Luke will not go to jail for borrowing from the education fund, but he is morally wrong.

As angry as Blair, Joyce and Valerie may be about how poorly their husbands handle tempers or the family finances, the quick fix of threatening to retain an attorney is no solution. Such action or threats cannot be made or taken lightly, because legal action creates a deep breach in family relations.

In instances where something may be morally and spiritually wrong but not legally wrong, the threat of suing, getting an attorney for every little moral ruffling of the feathers, is both immature and unchristian. There is no quick fix to right legal and moral wrongs. Attorneys are interpreters of the law and are not the quick fix for marital problems.

Even if a couple doesn't settle difficulties through an attorney, people find more subtle ways to rely on a quick fix. These alternatives offer ways of ducking problems rather than standing up and facing them squarely.

Marsha, for example, is a very bright and capable woman. A college graduate, she has engaged in several short-lived career efforts. Her impulsive job-jumping is a source of deep frustration to her husband, Jeff, who works hard to make good money. During the past five years, Marsha has become active in a charismatic church group. She's given up her latest job in order to create time for the Bible studies, to help her friends and to care for her children. Marsha claims her last job created too much pressure, and instead of looking for another job, the easy "quick fix" is her church group. She tells herself she does not have time for a job because of her other activities. Marsha has developed an inappropriate way of confronting her immaturity. Quick fixes are rarely lasting solutions, and her marriage is in trouble.

Jeff is a high producer in his successful business. Charming and known as a womanizer for years, his marriage to Marsha was seen by all as a step toward maturity and stability. However, most of Jeff's work colleagues find their quick fix to relieve stress in their recreational activities: racquetball three days a week, golf or boating on the weekends in the summer, and skiing in the winter. Jeff works hard to support his family, to cover alimony costs from a previous marriage and to maintain peer-induced recreational activities. Therefore, he is never around the house, his wife or his children. His quick fix is sports. Jeff's deadlock arises because his emotional marriage is more to his work and recreation than to his wife.

Marilyn, sixty-five, is in her third and now rocky marriage. She is whole-heartedly devoted to her church group and adores her three children from her first marriage and her five grandchildren. Simeon, her current husband, is an independent businessman. Essentially they go their own ways. He works long hours, loves his work and is active in civic organizations both locally and statewide.

Marilyn gets lonely easily, and when she wants company to pass the time she reaches out to Simeon. Because of Simeon's work habits, Marilyn complains bitterly that he doesn't support the marriage. He complains she doesn't want him around, especially when her children and grandchildren are present. The core of Marilyn's problem is that she wants Simeon around as a quick fix only when she feels anxious and lonely. Between her church and family there are few times when she feels any need for her husband. But by then she's tired, anxious and generally disgruntled. Obviously he can do nothing right in her eyes, and following holidays she becomes more upset. Invariably she threatens to call her attorney to divorce Simeon because he won't do things her way. But she gives little to the marriage.

In Marilyn's marriage, she wants everything perfect for her. She wants her children and grandchildren to be happy and her husband to be gainfully employed and self-fulfilled. She wants to stay active in her teachers' association, the local arts' council and her church choir. She wants to guarantee to everyone she knows that everything will always work out and that no one will be disappointed. She wants a money-back guarantee to life and marriage. So the more disappointment she feels, the more she is certain someone else is cheating her—her husband through his work; her children in their responsibilities; and her grandchildren who are irritable because they don't spend enough time with their parents. Marilyn must learn money-back-guaranteed marriage relationships exist only in fantasy land. They are quick-fix promises that cannot be delivered.

I Want My Way

In these illustrations each individual claims a sense of entitlement: "I deserve the marriage my way." The actual marriage relationship is secondary. The real commitment is to activities and people outside and beyond the marriage. The claim that "I'm getting an attorney" or "I'm going to play golf" or "I'm having the children over for dinner" or "I'm going to the healing service" are interchangeable excuses for not being willing to put the marriage ahead of personal desires.

Sometimes a quick fix involves placing excessive demands on the partner, instead of developing interests outside the marriage. Buddy claims that he's the head of household. To hear him describe how he "runs his house," it's clear he doesn't give good spiritual leadership. But in a more powerful and more destructive attitude, he thinks Joyce must be his mother. This is not a case of incest; it is a way of getting a quick emotional fix from the marriage. Buddy wants Joyce to baby him and becomes angry when she won't simultaneously be wife, lover and mother for him.

Jack has a better emotional partnership with his wife, Sharon, but he has not made a mature shift from his fantasies of the All-

American professional athlete to being a husband, father and worker whose main way of life is not lived on the athletic field. Twenty years after concluding his playing days, he still fancies himself a professional "jock." Competitive sports, not his marriage, is what excite him. Sharon is expected to be a confusing blend of supportive mother and passionate cheerleader.

Wilbur has had two wives and at least an equal number of affairs. Currently he is married to a divorcee with two pre-adolescent daughters. Outwardly, Wilbur and Heidi appear deeply in love. They are active in church, and Wilbur is extraordinarily supportive of his daughters' activities in gymnastics, scouting, church and school. Wilbur's own sons live out-of-state with their mother. In the interim between his marriages he had moved in with his mother, who was more than eager to provide a maternal quick fix for him. She took him in, comforted him in his marriage breakup and looked the other way during his affairs.

Moving from his mother's house into his new wife's house seemed liked a natural and effective transition for Wilbur. But his emotions didn't follow the furniture. Because Heidi had to raise her children as a single parent for a number of years, her sense of efficiency and mothering skills had become highly polished and effective. Inevitably, conflict soon arose between Wilbur and Heidi. Rather than stick it out in their house, Wilbur found it easier to escape his and Heidi's deadlock with a quick fix: moving to mother's home and her all-encompassing acceptance.

Eventually Heidi and Wilbur both realized that the quick fix of escaping to his mother's place could not possibly help their marriage. Wilbur has to decide where he is going to live and to whom he is going to be married. Heidi will not support him in the way his mother does. He will have to grow up and become an adult. That means accepting fewer quick fixes and easy escapes.

Harassment as a Quick Fix

Leslie found another type of quick fix when word leaked back that her husband, Robert, was having an affair with a fellow employee. Leslie's father is a detective who coached her well on how to conduct an investigation. Soon she had the goods on Robert! She had seen him and the woman behaving affectionately in public, and she compiled a fairly accurate and lengthy list of times and dates that Robert's car was parked at the woman's house. More work secured the woman's unlisted phone number. Pretty soon a barrage of "quick fix" harassing phone calls flooded Robert at work. They followed him to his new apartment, to which Leslie had exiled him, and then to the woman's place.

Married for a number of years, Leslie and Robert have two college-age sons, are prominent members of the local church and are involved in a variety of civic activities. In short, they are well respected. The idea of Robert being involved in an affair is more than Leslie can stand. What she doesn't realize is that she has made matters worse by continuing to harass her husband, his mistress, the police, her pastor and their friends. Her tactics provided her with a quick fix: they exonerated her and fueled her anger at being wronged. She wanted to gain sympathy for herself and get Robert back, but the opposite has happened. Instead, she has destroyed her husband's respect for her and made herself appear an undesirable nag. Now Leslie is an object of a legal threat as a result of pestering "the other woman." She is an emotional basket case in her pastor's presence and is shunned by her more discerning friends.

Legally and morally, Leslie is right. But the quick fix harassment technique usually produces exactly the opposite of the desired effect. In harassing Robert, Leslie believed that the solution to their marital problem was very simple. Robert must get out of the apartment, quit seeing the woman, move back in with Leslie and stay under her thumb and eyesight one hundred percent of the time.

Robert must end the relationship. This *is* the first, necessary step. But it is a quick fix. It doesn't remove the reason he became involved in the illicit relationship, and it does not break the marital deadlock to bring reconciliation between Leslie and Robert. Leslie must realize that nagging will not bring about the break-up of Robert's relationship and will not break up their marital deadlock. She must be willing—as must Robert—to accept blame for her own wrong-doing if she has any hope of mending the relationship.

Sometimes church groups, country club memberships and running home to mother become quick emotional fixes which may give temporary comfort to one partner. These "solutions," however, become excuses for not facing the real marriage deadlocks and prevent healing.

Questionable, if not unscrupulous, attorneys wait for accidents to happen, then quickly offer their services. In the trade they are known as ambulance chasers. Several years ago an airliner crashed during take-off from Detroit's Metropolitan Airport. The fire trucks had scarcely sprayed foam on the wreckage before legal counselors came out of the sheet metal and smoke promising to help the bereaved families—for a fee, of course. One can fault legal ambulance chasers. But we should also be wary of marital ambulance chasers—the attorneys, mothers, children, illicit lovers and golfing partners who offer disastrous quick fixes for marriage problems.

To review, the worst of the quick-fix efforts is expressed by the threat "I'm getting an attorney!" That response is a certain sign of a deadlocked marriage in which a divisive, if not irreconcilable, schism exists. Lesser forms of the quick-fix syndrome also persist in Christian marriages. These unchristian, unloving and immature actions create the exact opposite of their desired effect. No one has a quick fix to heal anger, broken relationships, affairs, wrong-doings and disappointments. When the words "I'm getting an attorney" are hurled into the midst of a relationship, it is a sure sign that somebody's reaching for the ultimate marital quick fix.

Christian Truth:
The Law Destroys; the Spirit Builds

When they threaten to get an attorney to settle deadlocked wedlock, most people do not realize the destructive nature of that step. Instead of breaking the deadlock, they are building a roadblock to reconciliation. You see, the law destroys and divides. It doesn't build or provide positive judgment. Its legalism doesn't heal; only the Spirit does that. It may be necessary in some cases to get a lawyer, but generally the law divides instead of bringing healing.

The law exists to protect the rights of individuals or groups from behavior that violates those rights. It is based upon evidence of actions, not thoughts or feelings, and exposes the specific effects of our behavior.

The law is also arbitrary, not directly concerned with motives. It seeks to determine damages. Spiritual reasoning is more subjective and requires a different thought process from coldly objective legal reasoning. Trying to solve marital conflicts through legal means is at best problematic, but more typically it spells disaster.

For example, if you have lived with a spouse for an extended period, you may be absolutely convinced of his or her sexual "monkey business." However, the judgment of the law is not based on perceptions but upon actual "wrongdoings" that can be verified.

The attorney's job is to focus on documentable behavior. In the final analysis, all attorneys are like Sergeant Joe Friday from the "Dragnet" television series. All they can work with are "just the facts, ma'am." Regardless of what one may have hoped for, such intervention in a marriage relationship always recasts everything in documentation. The questions attorneys ask are, "Can you document that your husband was involved on the telephone with the 'woman'?" and "Do you have long distance telephone logs?" and "Do you have the cancelled checks your wife wrote to him?" and "Can you produce credit card slips that show that on such and such a date your husband or wife signed a credit card voucher at an out-of-state establishment that coincides with the time that you claim the affair was going on?"

The law does not concern itself with the numerous times that you may have helped tuck your partner in after a depressing night, a bout of over-drinking, a long discussion that meandered through confusion and heartbreak. Those sharing of fears, woes and uncertainties are important. But once in the attorney's hands, the moral and spiritual values are separated from what the spouse actually did. The law drives a wedge between what one thinks and feels and what one has done.

The legal system exists to uphold the statutes of the people. But by the nature of its responsibility to look at behavior, it necessarily divides reality in ways that often are painfully and frightfully altered from the wording of the spouse filing the complaint. A legal settlement will never resemble a non-legal correction of a grievance. There is no quick fix. Getting an attorney makes a reasonable solution even more difficult to achieve. It may be necessary to retain an attorney, as was the case with Phyllis whose drug-abusing ex-husband perpetually reneged on child support payments. Still, it will never be a quick fix. It will always be painful and costly, leaving permanent scars regardless of who was right or wrong. It is much better and scriptural to discuss difficulties before calling the lawyer.

While Blair was in the process of seeking legal separation, she and Earl were open enough to the Holy Spirit to seek spiritual counsel. The Spirit invites reconciliation. There is always the possibility that if we reason together as Christians we can work through our problems. A couple may well need a period of physical separation, but coming together and reasoning with spiritual counsel avoids the quick-fix myth that legal separation papers will bring a couple together and not drive them apart.

Doug and Nancy have been married for twenty-three years

and have two sons, one a college football player and the other a tall, junior high school basketball player. They are a delightful couple and pillars of the church and community. However, Doug and Nancy struggle over his infatuation with a recently divorced young woman. When Nancy first found out about Doug's affair, she wanted to grab the quick fix of an attorney.

Prayerful consideration made her change her mind. Initially, she sought counsel from her pastor, who then invited both Nancy and Doug to come talk over their marital problem. By being able to talk and argue in a neutral environment, they began to reason together. The probability of keeping their marriage together is high because they have allowed the Spirit to invite them to come and talk together.

The Children Can't Help Us

Perhaps the more difficult invitation of the Spirit is the invitation of the children to be involved in working out family and marital problems. Many couples believe they should not involve their children in their difficulties. However, if the children are in adolescence or older, they already know what's going on and, in fact, feel neglected if they are not included. It is embarrassing for parents to share their marital deadlocks with their children. Now the reason for sharing difficulties is not to increase parental embarrassment or to overwhelm children with the facts of the marital life. Children can be of help if they are graciously and thoughtfully invited into the discussion. It is a matter of trusting God's Spirit to invite husband, wife and children into a marriage problem-solving relationship.

Still, when attempting to resolve difficulties, it is difficult to become vulnerable to a person who has hurt you. Then too, at times a situation seems so hopeless a couple is unwilling even to try to break out of the deadlock. At the time of Jesus' ascension into heaven, the disciples initially were enveloped in a sense of hopelessness about the future and direction of the church. Jesus had promised a Comforter and assured the disciples that they would not be left alone. The same invitation comes to the Christian family. We will not be abandoned in our current dilemmas. The Spirit invites families to look beyond the events of yesterday and the confusion of today into the joy and reconciliation of tomorrow. It is not a matter of simply saying that time heals all. Time alone doesn't heal; the Holy Spirit invites us to move beyond the heartbreak of the moment and facilitates that healing.

The Call to Honesty: "Speak the Truth"

While the law may divide, the Spirit judges, and the Spirit's judgments are a two-edged sword. The Spirit calls us to tell the truth. When a family member has been involved in legally questionable activities (i.e. adultery, embezzlement, non-support, abuse, incest), the words of truth about those activities are hard to confess. But the truth must be spoken. The words must judge the behavior in order to go beyond it. That's one reason we refer to Jesus as the Word become Flesh. God's word of love was spoken. We are called to speak the truth in love. We are called to say the words that may be most painful: "I'm sorry." "I committed adultery." "I took the money from the account." "I had sex with my daughter." "I lost my temper and got out of control." Healing cannot occur unless the words of truth are spoken in an atmosphere that invites one to confess the truth.

Once words of truth are spoken, the Holy Spirit intercedes to judge the motive and offer understanding. The Holy Spirit intercedes with something much more profound than human understanding to provide spiritual understanding between husband and wife, parents and children or between people outside the family with whom either spouse may become sexually, financially or legally involved. The Spirit judges the rightness and wrongness of our relationships to provide us understanding and acceptance of the wrong-doer.

The Holy Spirit also calls us to probe to the bottom of our problems. We have to penetrate below surface injuries, injustices, bad attitudes and immoral actions and find the depths of why people do what they do. As long as we are content to stay on the surface, God can't help us. We must be willing to probe to the core of a problem. Once the core is located, transformation and renewal are not far behind.

By its design, the law divides. When we think we are right, we want to believe the law is our best companion. And it may be! But the law always divides reality differently than we experience it. If we trust the Holy Spirit, not the law, to bring about reconciliation, our first action is to ask the Holy Spirit to invite us to come together to help work through the wedlock deadlock. Next we must trust the Spirit to judge us so that the root of the problem is exposed. Then the process of healing may begin. The next steps of healing, blessing and transcendence are possible.

After the problem has been detected, it's time for healing and rebuilding. The healing process begins with *words of confession*. The Scripture reminds us, "if we confess our sins, [God] is faithful and just and will forgive" (1 John 1:9). The Spirit cannot heal until we offer words of confession. Those words must come from *all* parties concerned: husband, wife and perhaps, children. The confession may be of acts done, deeds suppressed, attitudes aggravated, feelings festered, resentments encouraged or bitterness nurtured. God promises that as words of confession are offered to him and to one another, the Holy Spirit *will* heal.

Then, if spiritual values are to be central to a marriage, the family must go beyond words of confession to *words of repentance*: "I am sorry for working too long." "I regret avoiding the family." "I am truly sorry for committing adultery." We "all have sinned and fall short of the glory of God" (Romans 3:23). Still, the Spirit cannot heal unless we repent of specific activities and thoughts. Unless there is repentance both toward God and family members, the Spirit cannot heal.

Once confession of specific activities and attitudes is made, and repentance offered with a genuine and contrite heart, then *words of forgiveness* must be offered to each family member. We can never simply forgive and forget. What has happened has happened. The words of forgiveness are not words that dismiss an activity. We dare not try to pretend or deceive ourselves that history has not occurred. What has happened is fact, and in the final analysis cannot be forgotten.

Forgiveness does not make an event go away. Forgiveness is the Holy Spirit's way of enabling us to begin to *remember what has happened in a different way*. Remembering differently releases resentment, anger, self-righteousness and guilt. Through words of forgiveness the Spirit heals, enabling family members to remember their history in a new and different way, thereby creating a family's holy history.

If confession, repentance and forgiveness are offered individually and jointly within the marriage, the Spirit begins healing actively. As healing occurs, the marriage is centered in spiritual truth and thereby receives the Spirit's blessing in the following ways.

1. Offering Power to Continue

Scripture preserves for us the creation story, including Adam and Eve (Genesis 1-2). God made human beings as the crowning act of the wonders of six days of creation. The uniqueness of Adam and Eve is threefold: (1) unlike the rest of creation humanity is made in God's image as companions for God, created a little less than God (Psalm 8:5) but in covenant relation with God; (2) God created Eve as companion for Adam and correspondingly to enjoy a covenant relationship with God; and (3) God created Adam and Eve—our progenitors—with free will.

Our fallen image coming through original sin can be restored by God's grace offered through Jesus Christ to those who receive it by faith (Ephesians 2:8-10). The Holy Spirit is present to enable us, as human beings, to reclaim, re-establish and renew the daily walk with God—the covenant relation given first as a part of creation (Genesis 2) and again in Jesus Christ.

Our primary commitment as Christians is to the covenant relationship offered through Jesus. As our commitment to that relationship is honored by the Holy Spirit, we are invited to the commitment to "dwell deep" (Jeremiah 49:8) in Christ, to enjoy the deep companionship with him. As we find strength to live out our commitment to God through Christ, sustained by the Holy Spirit, we gain the power necessary for the spiritual commitment to marriage. This is a higher and deeper commitment than the social and sexual commitments that provide the supporting strength for the Christian's commitment to marital fidelity.

It may appear that life cannot go on for a guilt-ridden individual driven to the edge of despair. A couple in conflict may fear for their marital future because of adultery, embezzlement or other immoral behavior. The gift of the Spirit blesses and gives power to continue on terms that may seem impossible. If confession, repentance and forgiveness have occurred, the Spirit gives power to stay in the relationship and thereby to heal the marriage.

2. Offering Power to Persevere

Beyond a commitment to continue in the relationship, the Spirit promises us power to persevere in the face of adversity and to regain our footing. The Holy Spirit empowers despite our feelings of revulsion, of wanting to hide and of wanting to avoid going back into the relationship. The Spirit blesses renewed commitment to marriage and offers the power to persevere.

3. Offering Power to Conquer

The Spirit gives spiritual wisdom and energy to continue in a relationship, but God also promises power to conquer. It is not enough simply to stay in a marriage. The real blessing occurs as we conquer fears, insecurities, defeats, betrayals, denials, obsessions, addictions and the breaches of faith. These negative activities and attitudes can and must be conquered.

4. Offering Power to Triumph

The Spirit promises to bless us for a triumphant life. Life is more than persevering in a relationship. We are promised victory and triumph. If we are faithful in the earlier stages of persevering, God promises that we will be triumphant in all aspects of our marriage relationships. That power is ours, and it is built upon the foundation of the Holy Spirit's healing and conquering power.

The law sets foundations; the Spirit deepens them. The marriage ceremony is a spiritual and legal cornerstone upon which the secure marriage is based. Just as one must pour a foundation before building a house, people must understand that marriages must have legal foundations regardless of how deeply in love they might be. The law sets the foundation, and the Holy Spirit offers to deepen it to the inner core of our spiritual lives. We are wooed in marriage by the Holy Spirit. The law cannot guarantee a clean heart, a pure mind or positive motives. Only the Holy Spirit can establish fully the will and power of God's salvation in our marriages.

The law also sets boundaries, while the Spirit gives guidance. The Ten Commandments given to Moses were the spiritual foundation blocks of ancient Israel. They establish general boundaries of human conduct. When Jesus was born, the boundaries of the law were so elaborate and confusing that the Scribes and Pharisees on numerous occasions tried to entrap Jesus in the law's endless maze. But Jesus, filled with the Holy Spirit, transcended those boundaries, giving spiritual guidance that did not destroy the law. Rather, he gathered up the law, summarized it and put it in its place.

The practical boundaries of life are established by the law. But we do not live by boundaries alone. Jesus, through the Holy Spirit, intercedes to give guidance in transcending the boundaries, offering more abundant life.

The law is concerned with actual behavior and activities. It is based upon agreements, transactions, covenant agreements and a commitment to certain kinds of behavior. But the Holy Spirit transcends those transactional agreements. The Holy Spirit gives *agape*—the selfless love for another that transcends behavior, agreements and negotiations. It is a free-flowing, deep-giving love that can only be empowered by the Holy Spirit (1 Corinthians 13).

In Sum

We need to remember that God is more than willing to help put our marriages back together, to heal, to bless and to transcend. But we have to offer words of confession, repentance and forgiveness. We must be open to the blessing to receive the power to continue, to persevere, to conquer and to triumph. God offers us transcendent victory in our marriages. We must be willing to go deeper than marriage agreements; we must be open to receive the guidance that the Holy Spirit gives. If we are to be finally victorious, we must transcend mere human love. Receiving the gift of *agape* love, we are empowered to break out of our wedlock deadlocks into the fullness of God's love for our marriages.

Six

We've Simply Grown Apart

Popular Myth:
Things Should Get Easier
as We Get Older

Christian Truth:
Cast Your Nets on the Other Side

Popular Myth:
Things Should Get Easier as We Get Older

We like to think we grow old gracefully and believe that life will treat our marriages kindly, especially if we try harder. That idea is based on a popular myth that time heals or redeems everything. However, we must not trust our marriage dreams to time and familiar patterns alone.

The Christian truth is that God constantly calls us to do things differently, to trust him and believe that in each marriage it is possible to cast our nets on the other side of our past and be blessed.

We do not dig ruts in a marriage by doing something once. Years of erosion slowly transform the little gulleys of marriage into holes of Grand Canyon proportions. A spouse may awake one day to find himself or herself at the edge of a marital precipice. Nancy, for example, called her pastor, choked up and unable to find the right words. Sensing deep distress in this lifelong member of the local Baptist church, her pastor encouraged her to catch her breath and go ahead with her story. Nancy and Doug have been married twenty-five years and have two college-age sons. Nancy has enjoyed her chores as a homemaker but is now actively re-involved in the work force.

Doug is a foreman at a company that manufactures sheet metal products. He's been employed there most of his married life. He is highly regarded by his co-workers at the factory. Their Christian marriage seemed secure. Embarrassed as much by her naivete as angered by her husband's moral breach, Nancy poured out her heart about Doug's affair.

As her story gushed forth, the pastor realized what bothered Nancy most about Doug's affair was the fact that she was totally unaware of the marital deadlock that led to it. Everything seemed to have gone well. There had been no major fights. No other men. No other women. They had always seemed able to work out their differences amicably. But, as Nancy put it, "We've simply grown apart."

Nancy was at wits end. Should she get a lawyer? File for divorce? Harass Doug? Run away? She has many options, but they all cascade into the bewilderment at the marriage falling apart. Nancy had failed to recognize the warning signs.

Yours may not be a twenty-five year marriage. It may be one of five, ten or forty years. Many Christian couples take too much for granted about each other. Finally one partner says by word and deed, "I can't take the marriage any longer; we've simply grown apart."

Older *and* Wiser?

This myth relates to the notion that "the older we get the wiser we get." Growing wiser may come with age, but it is not an evolutionary certainty either of marriage or of the aging process itself. In this chapter, I want to discuss some of the factors that contribute to this myth.

Many couples, married for a long time, may assume that their marriages are essentially secure. This assumption of security may relate to basic needs such as finances, sex, emotions and health. However, such an assumption may not be well-founded since one or more basic needs may be met while others are lacking.

Families fortunate enough to have relative financial security should be especially wary of assuming too much. Financial cares may be met, but the spiritual and emotional expense of living goes on. Not long ago I was having breakfast at a fast-food restaurant. I overheard two women, well into their retirement years, express concern about their financial problems. One woman said her house was paid for, and she was happy for that. But increasing property taxes meant her actual monthly tax bill was higher than her mortgage payments of twenty-five years ago.

No longer could this woman assume financial security. Her earlier logic was plain but now misleading: if a house is paid for, there will be no additional expenses. But she now has a high tax bill raised by inflation and property taxes. This sort of instability is not uncommon and can lead to emotional insecurity.

Don't take sexual security for granted either. Casually glance at grocery store checkout counter tabloids sometime. Or turn the dial to an evening or daytime television soap opera. It seems they represent what is becoming common in American society. The headlines and themes are crystal clear. The most susceptible age for having affairs is between thirty-four and thirty-seven for women; thirty-eight to forty-two for men. One may not safely assume that a husband or wife will look away from temptation when approaching the so-called mid-life crisis. The graying of America means that people live longer and retain good looks, sexual powers and a wistful eye later in life. Being forty-five, fifty, fifty-five or sixty is not a magic barrier that guarantees sexual fidelity. It is a false assumption that being married ten or thirty years guarantees sexual security.

Nothing for Granted

This is not to say we should learn to mistrust our spouses. The warning, however, is simple. I'm simply saying that we should not take our marriages for granted, as if they were operating on an automatic pilot. While a couple may appear to "get along" well, it doesn't mean the relationship is growing or maturing. For example, a husband and wife may learn a quality of being at ease in public with each other; their social skills may mature with age. We can assume that if one partner offers emotional security, both will feel more secure with the other. In time they better learn each other's idiosyncrasies and how to live with them.

Still, there is truth in the old adage, "Familiarity breeds contempt." The longer one lives with the emotional idiosyncrasies of a spouse, the more likely simply putting up with him or her may be falsely perceived by the partner as acceptance, ignorance or emotional support. Problems like snoring, picking one's teeth, having excessive body or facial hair, being myopic or even having a tendency to freckle easily, may be overlooked in the early years of marriage. One may be contemptuous of the other, but irritations are simply overlooked because more pressing problems consume the couple's energy. As life goes on, jobs stabilize and children move out on their own. Then the little mannerisms become magnified. The small problems may become large emotional barriers.

We all can think of couples who divorced after thirty-five, forty or even fifty years of marriage. "We've simply grown apart," they often say. It is more likely, however, that irritating habits, perhaps overlooked in earlier years, have become serious emotional barriers. A partner may be shocked to read a hastily sketched note left on the kitchen table seemingly out of the blue: "I'm not coming home tonight. I'm not ever coming home. I'll have my attorney contact you." Some notes are far less kind. We have no guarantees of another's commitment to our emotional security.

Health is another area of life people don't worry about early in marriage. We know people who brag about not having been a patient in a hospital since birth or since having their tonsils out. People take pride in their good health. They should. But good health does not extend indefinitely.

Not long ago I was reevaluating some life insurance policies. The agent observed that my Federal Aviation Administration medical certificate, which I have held for years and which requires a complete physical every six months, holds no guarantee of future health. "Paul," my insurance agent cajoled, "I don't think you can anticipate being more healthy in twenty years than you are now."

My first reaction was to argue. I've enjoyed superb health all my life. There was no reason it shouldn't continue. But twenty years would put me into retirement. I realized then I had a false sense of security. The agent was right. I was forced to look again at my assumptions about my health. I could expect more ambiguity about it in the future than I had had in the past.

Growing Apart

Our assumptions about the permanency of our security systems are based upon a popular myth: the older we grow, the less ambiguity and the fewer surprises we have to endure. But as life continues, it inevitably sows the seeds of surprises, often stated as, "We've simply grown apart!"

Another attitude that contributes to the "growing apart" myth is that honorable beliefs guarantee honorable behavior. This attitude, which I've divided into a number of sub-categories, can lead to disappointment, if accepted.

Mind Over Matter

This classic theological heresy pre-dates New Testament times and has been a constant challenge to the church. John's Gospel and his epistles address directly these Gnostic heresies. Gnostics believed in a secret knowledge given them by a "Redeemer God" that allowed adherents to oppose the creator god, the god of matter. The mind, they thought, was superior to the sinful body. The witness of John's testimony opposes secret theological knowledge. It is heresy to believe that salvation is given through a secret knowledge that rejects the trinity, by which God's redeeming Word is made flesh in Jesus Christ and by which God's sustaining grace is evidenced in the body faithful, the Church, through the Holy Spirit.

A commonly espoused belief in the United States affirms the heresy of "mind over matter." But good thoughts do not change facts. Honorable beliefs do not guarantee honorable behavior. The actual relationship of belief and behavior is more complicated than Gnostics teach.

Good Thoughts Get Good Results

The "power of positive thinking" fallacy lives on. Good

thoughts don't make a drought disappear. Positive thoughts cannot drive the stock market higher. Our best thoughts for children's success or for a meaningful marriage do not guarantee positive results.

Jeanie found this out the hard way. I had never seen her before she walked into my office. I was impressed by her poise. She looked like she had attended an airline flight attendant school or had been an instructor at a power-of-positive-thinking clinic. Everything about Jeanie focused on a positive image.

Less than two minutes after the office door closed, though, Jeanie was in tears. Her husband, Ed, was not behaving at all as she wanted. They are in their mid-sixties and have lived a normal, socially successful and spiritually upright life. On the surface there seemed to be nothing wrong. But as Jeanie and I talked it was clear that she could not conceive of why she and Ed may have simply grown apart. She has given her best thoughts and best intentions to their marriage. "How could anything other than good results follow?" was her frightening spiritual question.

The first consideration is the marriage itself. Jeanie is having to face painful realities that Ed has not followed in the footsteps of her good thoughts about him. It is still possible for them to get back on track, but for the moment Jeanie's life is shattered. The popular myth that a positive attitude about the marriage will produce positive behavior is crumbling.

A second consideration is the physical level of life. Research indicates that people who maintain proper weight and exercise programs can expect to retain physical strength and ability well into their latter years. But no direct extension of physical prowess extends from the forties into the eighties.

No amount of good thoughts will change that fact of aging. Many municipalities, track clubs and state organizations have various levels of senior competitors in golf, swimming, handball and the various track and field events. As one looks at the scores and recorded times, ten percent slippage in performance can be seen for each decade. It is unreasonable to expect someone eighty years old to perform at the same physical level as someone forty, no matter how positive the thoughts.

Positive Examples Reap Positive Followers

Sometimes couples become too angry, embarrassed or uncomfortable to talk about their problems. One spouse may conclude, "If I lead a good life, my spouse and other family members will follow my good example." That husband or the wife may rise early every day to care for the family, may be judicious about going to church and may make certain each day is filled with twelve to sixteen hours of hard work. The right music, magazines and books are always exhibited. The unspoken assumption is that if they set a good example in these important areas of life, the family members will follow. However, that simply is not the case. In some instances the vigorous establishing of positive examples serves only to irritate others and is in fact a source of quiet ridicule by other family members.

The good behavior of one spouse may or may not be contagious. If not checked, this popular myth that good works or positive attitudes over time will heal all may sooner or later lead to a martyr complex: "Because family members don't follow my lead, I must work harder. In fact, I am the only one in the family who cares."

One such martyr is Janice, a good Christian mother who tucks her children into bed with a good-night prayer. She loves them and wants them to praise the Lord for their health, family and daily events. Her children, being responsive, learned to pray and enjoy bedtime good-nights with Janice. But time moves on, and Janice cannot understand why her teenage children get into trouble with the police. As it turns out, part of the children's rebellion is against Janice's insistence on kneeling to pray with them at bedtime.

The intention is good, but eventually children have to learn to say their own prayers, in their own way, on their own terms and in their own words. The more that Janice insists on doing it her way, the more they "simply grow apart."

Michael, Janice's husband, loves his wife and is active in church. But he sees in Janice's religiosity an opportunity to abdicate his religious training and example-setting. If his wife takes the children to church, Sunday evening youth group and weekend trips—while he stays home to read the paper or mow the lawn—he believes his children will grow up religiously mature. As time passes, the effective rituals of earlier years fade and grow empty. Sunday school may lose its appeal. Bedtime prayers may be intrusive.

The best of intentions and beliefs do not guarantee behavior. Other people have wills and they choose to exercise them differently than we would choose them to. That split between desire and behavior is often expressed in the heart-rending phrase, "We've simply grown apart." Often the problem develops because a couple was never that close and covered over its differences with pet phrases, positive thoughts, happy faces and good examples that disguised marriage deadlocks.

Maturity Comes with Pressure

As I mentioned at the beginning of this chapter, one cannot assume the magical appearance of discernment when a certain birthday rolls around. Growing older as a human being or as a marriage partner may simply mean that one is growing older. Age does not make one mature. Maturity is how one responds to pressure and transforms that pressure into productive activity and attitudes about life.

Take, for example, the magnificent performances of the Mormon Tabernacle Choir. During the four-year construction of that great tabernacle, 1863-1867, an architectural marvel was being created. Anybody could have gone into nearby mountains and found tall, strong, hardwoods to make the trusses for the Mormon Tabernacle. But the architect wanted a building that would grant an unrestricted view for the congregation and whose acoustics would not require a public address system. There were many mature trees on the slopes surrounding Salt Lake City. What made the tabernacle a beautiful work of art was that the wood was placed under tremendous pressure to form a dome-shaped roof. The technology used continues to marvel architects. Old, strong trees didn't naturally create that acoustically perfect auditorium. Success came in putting the wood under pressure to create a desired effect.

On the human level, simply spending time together as couples and having much in common does not mean that we "grow up." Maturity comes in learning to be flexible under pressure so that we become God's future work of art.

Often I counsel a husband or a wife who complains about ways in which they have grown apart. Their family activities have fallen into disarray, and their lives seem out of control. In short, their wedlock deadlock spells their blah feelings toward each other and life in general. As we examine their stories, a typical pattern usually emerges. As individuals, they don't discipline themselves to work at the job, to dedicate a specific amount of time for work around the house or to spend time in devotions.

Start the Day Right

One thing I recommend for marital and religious blahs is that the couple discipline themselves to get up ten minutes earlier each day for a period of devotions. Devotional guides generally take three to five minutes to follow. I do not ask them to spend a half-hour in deep meditation or to lay prostrate on the floor in a prayerful attitude, initially. Rather, mine is a simple goal: If you can get up ten minutes earlier and spend five minutes having devotions before doing anything else, the devotions become a time for reflection and meditation. That will set the tone for the day. Some individuals complain they are not early risers. Then my challenge is, "Is your marriage and your life worth trimming ten minutes from 'The Tonight Show' or 'David Letterman?'" The obvious answer should be, "Yes."

"Go to bed earlier so you can get up and spend some time with God," I tell them.

My goal is to develop an attitude of spiritual discipline for each day. If an individual or couple can discipline their routine for the beginning of each day, the rest of the day becomes more manageable. Life takes on new meaning and magic, and relationships are renewed. The simple act of a disciplined time will help tremendously.

Most of us resent discipline at one time or another. "It's too restrictive," we argue, or "I can't be myself and be disciplined." However, it is a dangerous religious and psychological teaching to believe that one can simply be oneself. As human beings we are not as gentle, as predictable or naive as the lilies of the field. At the beginning of the twentieth century, novelist Jack London made quite a name for himself by depicting the wild and vicious qualities of nature, spun around the stories of huskies, the Wild West and Alaska. His message was plain and should not surprise Christians: nature is not always kind. The idea of a natural selection, which says that the best survive, is not true. The teaching of original sin in Christian doctrine testifies to the fact that the human heart, left to its own direction, grows wild, not good.

The idea of selfishly pursuing one's goals independent of the partner has devastating ramifications in a marriage. A husband and wife may feel relatively congenial and content for long periods of time in encouraging each other "to do your own thing," but eventually the husband and wife begin to lose contact with each other and grow apart. It is not wise marital advice to encourage someone "simply to do their thing." Whether seen in Jack London's dog stories, in the Watergate scandal or in the Defense Department's bribery scandals, a lack of accountability leads inevitably to trouble.

Christian Truth:
Cast Your Nets on the Other Side

The biblical story of Peter and John who had been fishing all night but caught nothing (John 21:3-11) provides a wonderful example for maintaining relationships. At daybreak Jesus challenged them to go out deeper and cast their nets on the other side of the boat. The Scriptures tell us that their catch exceeded their wildest expectations. The central teaching of the story is faith. Peter and John did not argue with Jesus. They simply acted by faith at his request, and their lives were changed completely.

Many Christian couples need to cast their nets on the other side of their marital boat. I don't mean they should start seeking extra-marital adventures. They should instead be willing to grow in new areas, to take some new risks, to expand some new horizons.

"We've always done it this way," is a rallying cry for those who have fallen into deep, eroded ruts of rigid continuity. It's a sure sign that they've been fishing from one side of the boat for too long.

Janice's parents have a nice vacation home. For years she and Michael and the children have vacationed with her parents, her brother and sister. Michael and Janice have always cast their nets on one side of the family boat. Perhaps it is time to change plans. Why not go out deeper? How about touring a different part of the country? As a family unit Michael and Janice need to be with their children on vacation apart from the cousins, nephews and grandparents.

One could imagine Janice's puzzled response if Michael were to make such a suggestion. "Why do you want to change?" she'd probably retort. "We've always done it that way. I thought you were happy." Michael may well have been happy, but there are other things to do, other parts of the country to see, new activities to plan with the children.

If you want your relationship to grow, change plans. Go somewhere else. Cast you nets on the other side.

Launch Out

Launching out into different waters involves more than vacations. Elaine believes a mother's place is in the home. She loves her children. She enjoys cooking and takes pride in having her house always ready to welcome Bruce home from a day's work. But now the children are gone and married. Elaine finds herself chronically depressed and unhappy. She and Bruce are having more fights. Occasionally they become embarrassingly noisy, and they are spiritually dismayed because they fight over little incidents. Bruce's solution is to come home from work later at night and leave earlier in the morning. He finds himself withdrawing from his deadlock with Elaine by reading the paper and watching television more. This irritates Elaine to no end.

Perhaps Elaine should cast her nets on the other side of the boat. She could get a job, find new friends, and put some of her nurturing energy to work in positive ways.

The initial advice that Elaine might rejoin the work force was not well received. She was dismayed and hurt that her pastor would suggest that she abandon her role as homemaker since she has enjoyed it so much. However, this simple suggestion could very well break the marital deadlock of boredom.

Anita has a slightly different problem. Her husband, David, needs less sleep than she. Fortunately, he has a job in which he can put in some overtime, and the whole family benefits from this. Initially it was a godsend for Anita, who wanted to be able to sleep a little later in the mornings since frequently she would be up in the middle of the night with sick or nursing children. David seemed satisfied with a quick cup of instant coffee on the way out the door.

As Anita began to talk to her counselor about her unhappiness and lack of self-fulfillment, they discussed starting an exercise program. "No, I really don't do much of that. By the time I get up and get going in the day, I simply don't have time," she argued. So they examined her daily household and work schedule. It became clear that Anita's early morning time had shifted from being an opportunity to catch forty winks after a night's hard work with the children to simply sleeping in later and later. Her weight gain, chronic depression and feelings of worthlessness as a wife and mother could be quickly traced to the fact that she really does not need the extra sleep.

Anita needs to develop an exercise program, and getting up with David would be the perfect opportunity for her to cast her marital nets on the other side. She doesn't have to prepare a breakfast for him, but ten minutes of just sitting together around the breakfast table sharing whatever comes to mind would be important for both of them. This would give her a chance to wake up, begin circulating and enter into a brief but rigorous exercise program. A very different and positive perspective on life is in store for Anita if she will put her early morning time nets down on the other side.

Too Much Church Work?

Eleanor and Brad's problem is not uncommon in evangelical families. They had grown up in the church and met at a small church-related college. Their marriage seemed made in heaven. They loved each other. They loved the Lord. They deeply loved their children. They took their roles as Christian parents seriously and made certain their family went to Sunday school and church and that the children participated in youth group and attended evening worship services. There was the Wednesday night service to attend also, and both Eleanor and Brad were on a couple of committees at church. Eleanor did not work outside the home, but she put in a lot of volunteer time at the church.

This good Christian couple expressed their frustration about how they were simply enjoying each other less. I quickly noted the total number of hours they were involved in church activities. My suggestion was simple and would seem a bit heretical. I asked them to put their nets down on the other side of their church attendance. Sundays had become too active and strained for this family. I suggested they go to Sunday school and church but make Sunday evening a family time. Like many devoted church families, it seemed that Eleanor and Brad preserved little time for their family to spend together. They needed some shared meals, walks in the park, playing ball, enjoying homework—simply being with each other. Their Sundays were consumed by church activities. Their Sabbath left no time for the family renewal itself.

I suggested they had a responsibility to care for their family needs before they were in a position to set a spiritual example for, or were free to take care of, others. They had not done that before. But, like the apostles Peter and John, they were willing to cast their nets on the other side and were equally amazed at the immediate improvement in quality of their family life. Such a change does not mean they never will cast their nets on the "old side of the boat" again but, for now, a radical change is needed.

But We've Never Done it that Way!

Faced with a change in habits or a new opportunity some couples say, "But we've never done it that way." Such reluctance can be traced to the fear of the unknown, and fear plays a part in the failure to cast your nets on the other side. This is especially true for Blair and Earl who are somewhat introverted. Their home has been their safe haven for them and their children. As their separate careers have developed, they have become aware and embarrassed that they are not invited to many parties as a couple. As we talked about their frustrations, I asked, "How many times have you invited a couple or a group of people to your home for dinner?" They shrugged, rather sheepishly indicating they couldn't remember the last time. We pursued this line of discussion, and I suggested that if they wanted to be invited out they needed to learn to entertain at home.

Blair protested faintly, "But we've never done that, really! Early in our marriage, Earl was so busy with graduate studies and career that we never got into entertainment." As the conversation progressed, both Blair and Earl agreed that, while they had never done it, they could entertain and would probably enjoy it. They would most likely feel better about themselves, and they would be invited to other people's homes and parties.

Fear plays a different role in Max and Cher's life. They have time for everyone else, including children, church, civic and professional activities. But the idea of going for a walk together at the end of the day, hand in hand, with no specific agenda, no telephones, no television, no recording machines or personal stereo, posed a frightening alternative. They had toiled all night with the nets of their family relations but had never put their nets down to make time for private walks together. They were fearful of the intimacy and the silences that being together would create for them.

I suggested that taking time devoted to their relationship could help them grow together. They agreed. Going for a walk is an easy thing to do, and it will help keep them from growing apart.

Can't Take a Vacation

Many professionals I know, including some clergy friends, are simply afraid to take a full week or two of vacation without being tied to their offices by the umbilical cord of the telephone. Admittedly, many of these parishoners are busy and have people whose lives depend on their skills and familiarity with the situation. But further conversations, especially discussions with secretaries and other staff associates, indicate that many of these pastors call back because they are bored, a bit insecure and uncertain that the business can get along without them. Perhaps they are fearful that it will get along *better* without them!

There's nothing more frustrating to a spouse than to have a husband or wife on a vacation continuously running to a pay telephone, returning calls in the middle of the night or chatting with colleagues.

Recently, on an out-of-town trip and seated by myself at a restaurant, I couldn't help but overhear a conversation among four businessmen preparing for a meeting the next day. One of these men, a regional manager, had just purchased a portable Fax machine. He was delighted that he could plug his latest administrative plaything into his car, boat and, teased one colleague, his airplane. I thought, *How burdensome it must be never to be away from the business.* How easily the latest plaything or over-attentiveness to business can drive a wedge in a marriage relationship.

There's no reason why a business can't run itself. There's no need to toil day and night. That is truly an example of putting the nets down on the wrong side of life.

Paul doesn't have trouble "calling home" when he leaves the office—he's afraid to leave it at all! Paul and Frances have been married a number of years. He is a successful surgeon in a medium-sized general hospital. The marriage has fallen on difficult times because he is always at work. Colleagues, nurses, staff and former patients testify to his sensitivity, skills and availability. Everyone praises his care and concern—except his wife and children. For years Frances has been pushing him to take on an associate at the hospital or to move to a clinic or to a larger city where he could be on a rotation schedule, give the family some quality time and begin to enjoy the fruits of his labors. But he won't.

It's clear that Paul is "Saturday's hero" at the hospital. He complains that he works too hard. But he won't give up his hero status. He fears losing this continuous reinforcement of his self-esteem which he'll have to share if he works with someone else. He doesn't have to toil all night. Bringing an associate on board or joining a clinic doesn't mean he would lose either personal or professional identity. It does mean that sharing the responsibilities and the glory would give time for Paul and Frances to grow closer together rather than further apart.

These ways to cast your nets on the other side of the boat will work in most cases, but they suggest scary possibilities for many people. One can only join with many who came to Jesus saying, "I believe . . . help my unbelief."

Take the First Step

Folks may be willing to take a first radical step of a life-changing decision but are scared what the second, third or fourth steps might mean. First of all, it is frightening to cast your nets on the other side. You simply may not have done it that way before; it's different and it feels strange. But this is a good sign because it means you are willing to place the nets on the other side of your boat, and you can change.

Sometimes we are afraid to shift to the other side of the boat because we may fear success. So the second truth is to overcome the resistance: "I'm afraid it will work! My previous rituals, activities and ways of doing things may not be needed anymore." Believe that there actually may be a better mousetrap. There may be renewed life and vitality in your marriage, in your life and in your future. Change itself makes one fearful, but you must take the first step.

A third kind of unbelief at the heart of every radical step of change is: "I can't control my future." Radical faith means that we don't control our future, but we trust someone who can. Mary Magdalene, once possessed by demons before encountering Jesus, was faithful to be with Christ at the cross, and she was the first to encounter the empty tomb. She had been controlled in her past; she knew that she couldn't control her future. In becoming a follower of Christ, she took the first step of radical belief. It is radical to cast life's nets on the other side when we can't control the nets or their catch. So, it comes down to a question of radical trust.

Couples who have been through difficult times, raised children and faced an uncertain future are better prepared to accept Christian truths for changing their lives. They have had to adapt to much anyway. They are open to confessing their unbelief, their weariness from toiling all night and are ready to go out deeper and put life's nets down on the other side of their past.

Some couples have not learned to expect good things because they've agreed to toil all night on the wrong side of their relationship. They don't believe they have anything positive to celebrate.

So we must look, briefly, at ways in which the relationship can grow by learning to receive.

Take Hold of the Romance Offered

My wife and I grew up in an era when dancing was not a positive hallmark of the Christian. Therefore, neither of our families did ballroom dancing. One of the romances my wife has offered me is to learn to dance. It's easy for her! She's trained in music and has a good sense of rhythm. I can scarcely carry a tune in a basket. It is awkward at mid-life to take hold of the challenge to learn to dance for fun, relaxation and romance. But learning to dance is the romance and the risk offered. It will be fun and will draw us together.

Take Hold of Maturity

We can do many things if we believe that we have learned some things from which other people could benefit. One way to bring your marriage closer together is to volunteer for service jobs such as Sunday school class teacher, working with the youth program or perhaps volunteering for civic affairs. The list could go on.

Often people grow apart because they are bored, have low self-esteem and don't look beyond the end of their noses. There's a great new catch out there waiting for those willing to use their nets and enjoy the fruits of their labors. Be a Sunday school teacher. Be a scout leader. Be a driver for Meals on Wheels. Be a big brother or a big sister for someone.

Many couples have made a decision not to have children. In honoring that decision and in order not to come up with empty nets, these couples must make a self-conscious decision to help prepare the next generation. One doesn't have to have biological children to be a nurturing individual, but if a couple does not take on some responsibility to nurture others, it becomes a sure-fire way to grow apart.

Take Hold of Your Insecurities

One of the great promises that Jesus gave his disciples was

that *first of all* they were called to be disciples. They didn't all have to be teachers. They didn't all have to be prophets. They didn't all have to be missionary evangelists. They didn't let their limitations overwhelm and intimidate them; they admitted their limitations and adapted to them.

Peter did not have a formal education. Paul was well educated. Therefore, in reading about Peter's ministry we don't notice encounters with the Sanhedrin, high government officials and the intellectual elite. Peter's great catch was that he could be an excellent Peter; he was not called to be a Paul. Be pleased with the person God created you to be.

A family may have been committed to specific activity patterns: Christmas is *always* celebrated on Christmas Eve, Thanksgiving is *always* spent with her parents, Christmas is *always* spent with his parents. Often secret resentments build up over those "always" patterns, but no objection is offered because of the fear of offending. Instead, take hold of the insecurities, share the problem with each other, and decide as a couple what you want to do and what you are able to do based upon both positive commitments and acknowledged limitations.

Spouses must also admit insecurities to each other. For example, the husband may be a great fisherman and water enthusiast, whereas the wife hates water, can't swim and is easily sunburned. Learn to be who you are and allow your partner to help you become more secure. No one individual or marriage partner is called to be both Peter and Paul. We have different gifts and talents. God can use these differences to his glory if we will claim our insecurities so they can be transformed in our relationships.

Take Hold of Your Responsibilities

Being married and rearing a family is the most demanding and exhausting activity that humans can undertake. Many couples become resentful over the naivete they brought to the marriage. Instead, they should take hold of their responsibilities. That means being thankful for a loving spouse, shelter, food on the table and the challenges of married life. In their remorse, many desperately lonely single or single-again individuals covet the kind of responsibilities and corresponding joys that many marriage partners think too burdensome.

Be thankful you have children to send off to school, camp or to be with their playmates. Responsibilities are opportunities for growth, not simply ways to wear us out. One reason I insist that couples have table grace at mealtime is to encourage them to be thankful for simple, everyday things of life and to receive affirmation for the responsibilities they accept for their families.

If a couple takes hold of its responsibilities as a fresh catch on the other side of the boat, the reward will be great.

Take Hold of Your Possibilities

Perhaps you have a secret desire to be a missionary. Or you may have considered adopting a child, whether or not you have your own children. Perhaps, as a grandparent, you would like to be a youth advisor. All those possibilities present themselves and are limited only by whether you reach into the net of this new catch and take hold. Taking hold of the possibilities that you and your partner see will help you grow together because you have diversified your interests and commitments out of love.

In Sum

The radical call of the gospel is that we can turn our lives around and move in new directions. Spouses who complain they've simply grown apart also can reverse the direction of their lives and begin to grow together. The challenges and rewards will be great.

Seven

I'll Hang on 'til the Children Are Grown

Popular Myth:
I Can Hide Behind the Children

Christian Truth:
You Must Learn to Relate
to Your Spouse

Popular Myth:
I Can Hide Behind the Children

Deadlock may occur when a spouse uses the children as an excuse for not facing marital difficulties. Michael, for instance, clearly was bitter and angry as he unloaded his accumulated aggravations about his wife, Janice. In his heart he wanted to leave her and forget the whole situation. The words "separation" and "divorce" came slowly to his lips, but they were certainly clearly in his mind. The primary restraint on Michael's hopelessness regarding his marriage was his dedication to his children. He simply could not conceive of leaving until they were grown. Initially that took care of the problem, but it didn't save the marriage. If he were honest with himself he would realize he has no reason to stay in the marriage simply until the children are grown. There's more to life and marriage than being a caretaker for youth. There's fulfillment, renewal and the possibility of high-quality living.

Some people choose to avoid facing marital deadlock by blaming problems on the responsibilities and obligations of marriage. Children, of course, are part of those responsibilities.

To her friends, to herself and finally to her counselor, Jane admitted her adolescent lust for total freedom. She doesn't fancy herself a good housekeeper or a good cook, but she does perceive herself as a good mother. However, she believes Larry's irresponsibility has made her marriage one of heavy obligation and burden. When asked what she wants out of life and her marriage, Jane's thoughts turn to ideas and conceptions more appropriate for adolescent youth. She wants to live a carefree life, unfettered by responsibilities.

Part of growing up, with or without children, is learning to accept responsibilities. Other than taking care of herself, Jane gladly accepts responsibility for her children. The rest of married life is an undue burden. Jane has a considerable amount of growing up to do so she can dump her view that marriage responsibilities are simply burdens.

Anita, on the other hand, grew frustrated being only her children's caretaker. At first not having to answer the alarm clock, climb into a commuter car, hassle with parking, endure boring lunch hours and rush back home seemed like a fantastic deal for Anita. Married several years before having children, Anita was glad to swap motherhood for the mad, mad world of her career. However, their first-born was less than 18 months old when Anita began to realize this job of nesting might be all right for birds every spring. But birds build their nests, have young and soon send them flying on their own happy way. Not so for Anita. The nest obligations continue day after day, season after season, year after year, and she tires of them.

When Anita and David began to talk to a marriage counselor about her stifling nesting experience, she began to realize the problem was not just being married, having children or being at home. Whether one is the single, young career woman, a debonair partner in a dual-career marriage or a nesting mother, there are certain obligations that don't go away. Taking care of the two children is not the sole reason Anita complains of chronic depression, anomie and listlessness. In short, she wants few obligations in her life. Problems with children were only the tip of the iceberg for Anita and for David. Now the iceberg has been identified.

Children and Guilt

The biblical adage "be fruitful and multiply" is often used by parents and friends with children to make a childless couple feel guilty about not fulfilling a religious or patriotic duty to have children. Yet once the children come, the guilt doesn't go away. They have not accepted themselves as loving parents who want to have and raise children.

Many couples may feel guilty about having children. Then they live off guilt while staying in the marriage and raising their children. Both children and parents deserve more than guilty feelings.

Jane was angry at her husband and more so at herself because she felt trapped. She was mad at her husband for abandoning her and getting involved with another woman. But she resented most being stuck with having to take care of the children. To cope with her anger, she pretended that she didn't feel so guilty about not wanting to remain with the children. But at one point she admitted, "If the children weren't there, I'd be gone in a heartbeat! I really hate doing this all by myself."

Nancy, too, feels doubly guilty because her marriage is in trouble at precisely the same time she is endeavoring to launch a new, exciting career possibility that she loves. At a time when she's beginning to realize her career interests, she has to back up, re-group and nurture the children. This has provoked uncontrollable rage and guilt. Nancy doesn't want the kids to suspect how much she resents them, so she smiles a lot and goes out of her way to make them feel good. At the same time she feels even more guilt.

Adult Children

Sometimes adult children hide behind their parents. The bonds between adult children and parents who have been positive loving examples project an expectation of a happy successful marriage for the child. To disappoint one's parents with a divorce and custody assignments is devastating.

At one time I talked with a couple caught in exactly this dilemma. Kermit wanted out of the marriage, claiming he had been unhappy for a number of years. A successful businessman, he has the means to provide far more than adequately for his children, including college expenses and a suggested generous settlement offer. His wife, Laurie, knew that he was unhappy and was totally discouraged about the marriage. Kermit is an adventuresome, outdoors type; she the opposite. Laurie knows she simply cannot meet all his needs. She feels it would be better if the marriage were terminated, and we talked about the spiritual, emotional, financial and moral implications of such a decision.

The marriage survived for a time. Laurie redoubled her efforts to keep it together during her father's two-year bout with cancer. But no sooner had the dirt settled over her father's grave than she filed for divorce under terms to which Kermit had previously agreed. Why did the break-up finally happen? Laurie could not face divorce while her father was alive and seriously ill. She was gripped by hypocrisy each time she visited him, especially in the last six months before his death. Her father probably knew what she was doing and why and lived with his own guilt for not making peace with his daughter over her wedlock deadlock.

God Will Punish Me

Others will not face a deadlock because they fear God will punish them. Judy comes from a devoted Christian family. She herself is an active, born-again Christian, but severe problems exist between her and Joseph, her husband. Judy has a son and a daughter from the first of her three marriages, and her ties to the children are very close. Having "failed spiritually" in two previous marriages, Judy was determined, "come hell or high water," not to disappoint her children again. Her motives run much deeper than simply wanting to provide a secure family environment for her boys. She feels she is a spiritual failure to them, and she fears God will punish her if this marriage fails. Her guilt keeps Judy from being as active in church as she wants, and she doesn't go to Bible discussion groups because inevitably her marriage problems might surface and touch on her sense of failure as a Christian, a mother and wife.

It became clear to me that if her children were not around, Judy would probably not feel the overwhelming guilt that she is a disappointment to God. Her obsession with pleasing God and her children makes it nearly impossible to focus upon effective marriage problem-solving.

Another example of how husband and wife hide behind children is a belief that the kids can't take care of themselves or won't survive a divorce. Out of pity for the "poor children," a couple may stay in the marriage. But let's take a closer look at this aspect of the popular myth that barricades husband and wife behind children.

When Vickie and Frank first came to terms with the seriousness of their marriage difficulties, Vickie was absolutely convinced that the children could not survive the disruption and disillusionment of a marriage gone awry. A large measure of her protest against Frank, after he walked out one spring day, focused on the children whom Vickie believed could not survive without a father. Perhaps Vickie and Frank had been emotionally and financially overprotective of their children. Perhaps the children could well survive, however painfully, the emotional disaster of a separation and possible divorce. As Vickie and Frank became embattled over why they had marital difficulties, the issue of the children's defenselessness became "a red herring" in the arguments. Progress could not be made between husband and wife as long as the emotional weakness of the children became a pawn between them. Worrying about the children's emotional survivability, however humanitarian and sensitive that might appear, does not bring a couple back together.

Using Children as a Distraction

Blair and Earl wanted to spend more of their counseling session talking about the problems a split would bring to their children. They did not want to talk about themselves. It's easy to be evasive and distracted by things over which you have no control. Had Blair and Earl been half as loving toward each other as they were toward their children, their marriage initially would not have strayed into difficult times.

The couple's children are not small infants. They still have many important needs, and it would be nice if they could depend on stable, loving parents. But at the same time, Blair and Earl have retreated behind the defensive wall that "the kids wouldn't understand." On the other hand, Mom and Dad won't take initiative to help the children understand. Why? If the children understand the difficulties, they may challenge the parents to do something about them.

Sometimes children from previous marriages become convenient excuses not to face marital realities. Nell and Tommy have been married for a few years, and Tommy has custody of his daughter, Susie, from a previous marriage. His "ex" has since married a man with four children, one of the conditions of their marriage being that she would not bring Susie under their roof. Susie, therefore, feels obvious hurt from the rejection by her mother.

Nell and Tommy have a good handle on life, their idiosyncrasies and their marriage. The key source of their marital deadlock comes over Tommy's unyielding need to love, protect, overindulge and use Susie as a wedge between himself and Nell. Any time Nell raises a question about Susie's discipline, Tommy counters with the scenario of how she was rejected and needs to be loved. You can imagine how that makes Nell feel. Sooner or later it will be time for Susie to grow up and have a face-to-face conversation with Tommy about her mother and life with her stepmother. Tommy will be hard-pressed to summon the courage for that confrontation as long as he thinks Susie is defenseless and that he must love her more because her mother rejected her.

Render to Caesar . . .

Parents have substantial responsibilities in caring for their children. But their whole world cannot revolve around them.

When Jesus was presented a coin bearing Caesar's inscription, he was challenged to deal with a difficult dilemma. He was asked, "Who is your final authority? Caesar or God?" Jesus' response was disarming for them and can also be for parents who fight over their children. He said, "Give to Caesar what is Caesar's and to God what is God's" (Mark 12:17).

A question to ask yourself is, "To whom am I married?" An obvious answer would be, "my husband" or "my wife." A deeper issue is raised by this question, which is similar to the one put to Jesus. What is obvious is not necessarily most true. Often parents are married emotionally to their children. In psychological language, this is considered "co-dependency." We see its evidence in destructive patterns of alcoholism. A helpmate, a parent, a spouse or a child who is considered the "enabler" is bonded to the alcoholic. Rescuing the offender becomes a daily or weekly responsibility for the enabler. The co-dependence swings into effect when the problem drinker acts destructively in order to be rescued by the enabler. Co-dependency is like a self-destructive chicken-and-egg phenomenon after a while, as the enabler and the alcoholic reinforce each other's behavior.

Parents' emotional dependency on children is especially destructive. The question of "to whom are you married?" is a very serious one. In Judy's case, she is emotionally wedded to her son and daughter and is not about to allow any interference from her husband. She has not learned to render unto her children that which is theirs and unto her marriage that which is her marriage's.

What Would You Do to Salvage the Marriage?

Occasionally when I counsel a couple hiding behind their kids' emotional defenselessness and their own guilt about abandoning them, I pose a hypothetical question: "If there were no kids, and money were not a problem, what would you be willing to do to salvage the marriage? What would you want to do to make it work?" By posing this purely theoretical design for a deadlocked couple, they may come to see they are hiding behind the children. The Caesar of their children sets down obligations, commitments and loyalties which must be limited. Their main emotional commitments and obligations must be to one another. To make that commitment, one must purify marital motives about where and how priorities are established. This issue should be on one's marital good health checklist.

In many marital arguments, children become pawns in the conflict. They are manipulated by one parent or the other. But kids are far more perceptive than most adults realize, especially when they see moms and dads fighting with each other. Parents don't want to believe the children know what's going on and are players in the same game. Correspondingly, children may use a conflict between mom and dad to counter-manipulate. They play one parent against the other to get their own way.

Children as Hostages

In traditional, evangelical Christian families, with low incidences of divorce and marital discord, children may be openly used as emotional hostages. Because separation or divorce is not an open or popular option within evangelical beliefs, parents will battle over co-opting the children to line up on either parent's side of the family battleline.

Many parents do not realize how worldly-wise their own children are. Many of their peers and playmates have gone through divorces. A lot of the television programming centers around the exact problems, affairs and distrust that their own parents may be going through. The sociological virginity of many evangelicals gets them into problems with their children who have lost their cultural virginity about marital conflicts long before their parents.

Therefore, children become even more angry and counter-manipulative when they see their parents using them as hostages. The sad result is many parents' failure to realize two things: the viciousness of their hostage activity and the accuracy with which their own children perceive this hostage takeover. The popular myth promises parents they can use the children for personal marital gain in breaking successfully out of wedlock deadlock.

However, a first step for husband and wife in breaking such deadlocks is to behave as adults, not children, in marital conflicts. All of us bring some immaturity into our adult years and into our marriages. The sure sign that marriage partners have not grown up is when the husband or wife wants to process conflicts like an adolescent. When things go well, the adolescent mentality is fun, exuberant and delightfully irresponsible. When hard times come, the conflicts are difficult to resolve because neither husband or wife wants to view their interpersonal quarrels and squabbles as adult conflicts. They tend to encourage each other, the marriage relationship and their children to behave in a juvenile manner.

One cannot magically appeal to love, when day after day, week after week, one or another of the partners continues to behave in adolescent and irresponsible ways. Love may cover a multitude of sins, but it tires when pushed too far. This is precisely the point Jesus was making. As a citizen of this world, we cannot expect that all we have to do is render loyalty to God. Caesar must be paid. Loyalty to a marriage involves conducting arguments in an adult manner. Adults who infantilize their conflicts will predictably experience difficulty when helping their children with their conflicts and problems.

Christian Truth:
You Must Learn to Relate to Your Spouse

I try to warn parents who slyly, deliberately or perhaps totally unconsciously hide behind their children. I warn them that these behaviors are ineffective ways of restoring marital harmony. Hiding behind children makes one immature and childish. Even when children are not in the picture, couples often hide behind childish attitudes. The first task in breaking wedlock deadlock is to quit being so childish.

I readily recall couples with whom I have counseled where one or both partners have made serious omissions of behavior and attitude. When pressed, one spouse usually admits to hiding behind naive, childlike attitudes toward the marriage. In the heat of conflict, that person throws up his or her hands, saying, "It's all a game anyway. It really doesn't matter that much. This is all kind of silly."

Not a Game

Marriage matters. It's not a game. The naivete of little children belongs to little children. It is inappropriate for husbands and wives. Many who value their marriages highly are far more naive than they realize. As Christians they want to believe in the good, old time religion, a simple lifestyle, an uncomplicated future and a knowledge that things always turn out all right in the end. Those possibilities occur at times. But life is not easy and it is not simple.

As Christians we may have had parents, pastors and Sunday school teachers who lived and espoused the exact ideals we would like to follow. But we do not know the innermost secrets of their lives. Their experiences may have been more painful, and they may have been far less naive about the harsh realities of life than we recollect. There may have been a culturally and religiously sanctified naivete forty or fifty years ago. However, today's couple needs to put away childish things.

A delightful quality about children, especially those raised in a loving, nurturing Christian family, is a trusting perspective of life, God, the world, parents and reality. That's a blessing many people do not give their children. However, if we are not vigilant, we can allow a childlike sense of the world as a secure place to become distorted and unrealistic.

Often people who have come from dedicated Christian families believe the world owes them a secure existence. Many Christian couples deny they're in marital difficulty until it's nearly too late because, having grown up in a secure environment, they can't stand the thought of loss—loss of image, loss of ideal marriage, loss of a partner, loss of income. Theologically, such views don't wash. The world does not center on us. It does not owe us security. God is Lord. It is we who owe God allegiance and support. We must let God be God, let his world be his world. We find our security, not in what is owed us, but in walking by faith.

No Excuses

All of us, at one time or another, have stumbled over our childishness in making excuses. Some excuses are designed to explain away why we did what we did; others are used to deliver us from what we didn't do; and at times we use excuses simply to confuse others.

I have a friend with whom I have worked for many years in some difficult, ministerial professional relations. I overheard him put the issue of excuses to rest with this response: "Well, I will accept that excuse, because it's your best. I really don't want to hear your second best excuse." And life went on. But both my friend and his subordinate knew how childish and thin the excuse had been.

Unexpected circumstances may provide legitimate excuses, but most excuses are calculated to cover up something. One needs to learn to relate to the spouse by putting away excuses. Here are some frequently used excuses that need to be put aside.

"It's not my fault," is the classic childhood excuse we have all learned. The fault may be with an older sister, a younger brother or playmates. As adults we have carried stupid excuses to an extreme and see in them the terribly costly product liability suits. People willingly sue the manufacturer when they do not use common sense in handling the product. The rationale behind many of those suits is, "I don't want to take responsibility for anything I do. Any problem I have must be someone else's fault." Such an attitude spells disaster for a marriage. Problems may not be totally your fault, but to disavow completely any responsibility for your problems is immature and childish.

Because Nancy and Doug had been married for a long time when a strained deadlock troubled their marriage, Nancy was tearfully and regretfully convinced that there was nothing she could do about it.

Our initial response to a problem may be to act childishly, throw up our hands and say, "I can't do anything about it." But generally we can. It may be as simple as asking someone else, whether friend, pastor or professional counselor to help set us in the right direction. I believe there is nothing that we can't do something about. If there is, then it's not a problem or cause for complaint. That's part of why we have the community of saints called the church.

Another childish excuse we perpetuate is, "It isn't fair." Both before their marriage and continuing into the marriage, Wally had a reputation—one which earlier in his life he was proud to claim—for being a womanizer. His marriage to Jessica had been on rocky ground because of his frequent infidelity. She threatened to leave him, and for good reason, unless he quit his affairs "cold turkey." Jessica has an uncanny ability to know when Wally has been messing around, and ninety percent of the time she's right.

Finally, Wally made a commitment to be totally faithful to Jessica. And all evidence indicates he has been. Now, Jessica's work takes her out of town for frequent business-related trips.

Remembering full well the deception in which he was engaged for a number of years, Wally has become relentless in calling Jessica's room at night, making sure she engages in no suspect behavior. Jessica is behaving herself. But she claims that it isn't fair that Wally should be on her case all the time when she has never been unfaithful and doesn't intend to be. It's especially irritating since his history has been one of repeated infidelities and indiscretion.

Perhaps Jessica has a legitimate gripe. But not everything is fair in love or in war. It is better to have an over-conscientious, faithful, loving and concerned husband who may occasionally be insensitive and unfair in his marital detective work than one who is the opposite. Jessica must put away the excuse that Wally's response isn't fair, live out the turbulence of the present and get on with her life and her marriage. Maturity in learning to relate to a spouse is accepting that not everything is fair.

If we drop our excuses, we will always make some progress. Honesty, especially to oneself, is a sure foundation upon which to build a more secure and mature marriage relationship.

Black and White

Sometimes struggling to develop this maturity is difficult, especially if one or both partners tend to see everything without shades of gray. In counseling with some couples from traditional evangelical families, it's not surprising to hear the husband say that he has learned to see the whole world in black and white, right and wrong, left and right. Ultimately, of course, it is. But in the world, this side of heaven, there are many slips between the cup and the lip. Life is not a simple, straight-forward, clear-cut division between good and bad people, Christians and non-Christians, my fault and your fault. The first step in putting away immaturity is to realize that life is more complicated than we had imagined. We must accept that we walk by faith in a world colored by many shades of gray, with only an occasional glimpse of the essence of black and white.

Accepting a measure of grayness in life is not a matter of

weakness, it is a matter of growing up. If the law were sufficient for grace, there would be no need to walk by faith. The law would receive absolute compliance, and there would be no problems in life. But we live in a fallen world, and to be mature is to look at life in a more profound way.

To live, to be married, to be a parent, a citizen, a Christian and a human being, is to have responsibilities. Many Christian marriage partners accept too much responsibility for other people's behavior. That may explain some of the current revolt against accepting any responsibility—I am simply fed up with being responsible for everyone else. But Jesus says, "For my yoke is easy and my burden is light" (Matthew 11:30). Many people spend far too much money, energy and a good portion of their lives evading responsibility. They would accept themselves much more fully if they could accept the fact that to be mature is to be responsible.

Affirmation

Along with accepting responsibility, one must give and accept affirmation to be mature. Many times I have counseled couples who deeply love each other, and who would do anything for each other. But I sometimes note that the language of love and affirmation has become more and more intellectualized and less spoken. Occasionally I intervene in a discussion and ask either a husband or wife to turn to the partner, look him or her directly in the eye and say some specific word of affirmation. Then I turn to the other partner and ask him or her, "When you hear your partner saying an affirming word, how important is it and how good does it make you feel?"

This is a simple exercise, perhaps. But it's surprising how difficult it is for many of us to receive affirmation, love, appreciation and acceptance. It may be our attitude of works righteousness. It may be a kind of adolescent shyness about being told we're great. It may be the awkwardness of not being mature enough to receive loving affirmation from others. Whatever the root cause, it's fairly easy to change. A mark of maturity is being able to accept affirmation, especially from those who love us and appreciate us.

Having fun, yes fun, is a form of maturity. Enjoying humor and having a good time is far more than a distraction from the daily routine, and fun is more than being funny. It puts life in perspective and helps us to smooth ruffled edges. It's poetry.

The old adage, "All work and no play makes Jack a dull boy," is certainly true. Families must cultivate having fun and being spontaneous. Contrary to popular opinion, spontaneity, more so than sobriety, is the measure of maturity in our private and public lives.

Emotional and spiritual maturity are tied together. In addition to emotional maturity, which is basically an understanding of how the world functions, one must allow the Holy Spirit to develop qualities which make us spiritually, personally and interpersonally mature. There are many such qualities, but I will discuss a few of the most significant.

Agape Love

The key to the success of the gospel and St. Paul's teaching is recorded in 1 Corinthians 13, where we are invited to love with *agape* love. That is the simple, selfless love that has no thought or anticipation of return. This is the love that God has for us in Christ. It is a love born of heaven, not of earth. This is the most significant part of our behavioral maturity.

Commitment

In the marriage vows we commit ourselves to the other through thick or thin, for better for worse, in sickness and in health, children or no children. The commitment is there regardless of what difficulties or tragedies may come our way. Our commitment must be unconditional.

Patience

Christian patience means that we live through our frustrations. We are patient with ourselves, others and, above all, patient with God, since we don't always understand his ways. Our natural instinct is to be impatient, impertinent, testy and demanding. God, however, is extremely patient. We must draw on his patience to be spiritually mature.

Self-Acceptance

Self-acceptance is more than feeling good about ourselves and achieving a certain level of emotional comfortability. Self-acceptance means above all that we are accepted as a son or daughter of God. We are willing to go where the Lord leads us.

We recall Jesus' words to Peter that when he was old Peter would be taken where he didn't want to go because he was Peter, the rock on whom the church was founded. He was the head of the church of Jerusalem. He was the manager for the missionary travels of Paul. All this was made possible because he accepted himself as Peter and accepted God's call in his life.

In Sum

Anyone can become an obstacle to breaking wedlock deadlock—husband, wife, parent or child. Any possibility can become an obstruction. Any good intention can be maligned. The secret of the Christian marriage is for us to quit hiding, especially behind children. They provide so many opportunities for us to neglect our relationships with our spouses. We must accept the yoke of obedience and responsibility. That yoke is not negative and demanding. Rather it's one of mature responsibility that frees us to experience joy in our marriages.

Remember, over-solicitous concern about the welfare of our children does not always indicate genuine caring for them. Sometimes children's problems are symptoms of difficulties between husband and wife. Children alone aren't sufficient reasons for staying in a marriage, and they *seldom* cause a marriage break-up. As Christian marriage partners we must accept very seriously our responsibility to care for our children, but above that we must render to God that which is God's: the holy commitment to our marriage relationship. We can always take care of our children if we are able and willing to care for our spouses.

Eight

You Have to Peel Your Own Shrimp

Popular Myth:
Someone Else Will Take Care of Me

Christian Truth:
Pick Up Your Bed and Walk

Popular Myth:
Someone Else Will Take Care of Me

Many Christian men and women rail against the so-called welfare state. They cite chapter and verse to condemn folks who have been on welfare for years, pointing to their sloth and unwillingness to better themselves. They complain about the desire for a free ride and some people's unwillingness to take responsibility for themselves. However, many Christians fall into this popular welfare myth, except that they apply it to their marriages, not economics.

The Christian truth that counters the popular myth that "someone else will take care of me" comes from Jesus' words to the man who'd been brought through the crowds to Jesus for healing. Having performed the miracle, Jesus told him in perhaps an uncharitable way, "Pick up your bed and walk." The miracle was not the obvious one of medical rehabilitation, but that Jesus sent the healed man back into his community.

This Christian truth applies to marriages in this way. Day by day we must take responsibility for ourselves in order to be valuable marriage partners, integral members of the community and, above all, to glorify God. After all, God, through Christ, gives us the strength to pick up the beds of life and "to do justice, to love kindness, and to walk humbly with God" (Micah 6:8, author's paraphrase).

Marie and Don are a middle-aged couple who have been married off and on again for more than twenty years. They have not been divorced, but they keep having fights. Don leaves or Marie sends him away. After a time they get back together. It is a frustrating relationship and one that is not nearly as fulfilling as it could be.

Marie captures the essence of their marital problem with this story. She comes from a working-class family where she had little hope for a college education. As the middle of six children Marie learned housekeeping skills, especially cooking, at a young age. She had a touch for food preparation and liked it. By the time she was a teenager she knew she couldn't afford to go to college, so she used her creativity to develop a successful catering business.

Marie and Don were high school classmates and began dating midway through the ninth grade. By their junior year they were engaged and were married the summer following graduation. Don enlisted in the Navy and became a radar repairman. After leaving the military he was able to transfer his electronic skills into relatively stable employment as a television repairman in a hometown television repair service. Three children were born early in the marriage and are now on their own.

The capstone to Marie's frustration came one day when she was preparing for a client's party. She spent the better part of the morning peeling some fifteen pounds of shrimp for the afternoon reception, saving about a pound and a half so she could prepare a delightful shrimp salad for her own dinner. Perhaps other goodies would be left over from the afternoon's catering event. She imagined a pleasant meal and a relaxing evening with Don.

When she returned home at 5:30 she found Don, typically propped up in front of the television with a beer in hand and a suspicious-looking empty serving bowl on the floor next to his fully extended recliner. Closer inspection made Marie's heart sink and her blood pressure rise! Don had come home, opened the refrigerator, grabbed the whole pound and a half of nicely peeled shrimp and had devoured them with his drink. In turn, he was dismayed at her anger. Of course he had eaten the shrimp! They were peeled and ready, and he was hungry. It all made sense to him.

Marie tried to regain her composure while explaining to Don that his insensitive, greedy snack had ruined her day. He was incredulous. "After all," he blurted out, "didn't you peel them for me?" As she wheeled, angry and disgusted both at Don and at herself for having trusted him to behave, she shot over her shoulder, "Well, you're gonna have to peel your own shrimp from now on!"

Sins of Omission

Don had not done anything really wrong. The problem was he hadn't done what was right. For many Christians, both husbands and wives, their sins are those of omission, not commission. It's what they *don't* do that makes the marriage go sour.

Because Don's wife was the family entrepreneur and had a successful business, he believed he had no worries. He would never lose his economic virginity. A classic underachiever himself, Don could have started his own television repair business and done very well. He possesses all the natural skills and talents and is an outgoing individual. The Achilles heel of his marriage is his expectation that Marie will always peel his shrimp. Therefore, he is not concerned about providing well for his wife. She would like not to have to cater as many functions as she does, especially at Christmas. But Marie must meet financial needs during holiday times.

On his way to and from work, Don drives past several grocery stores. In the summer months he goes past small, roadside stands where he could buy fresh fruits and vegetables. Marie's work often requires her to be away during normal dinner hours, and she comes home exhausted. How nice it would be for Don to buy some food and have dinner waiting for her. But Don assumes that Marie will always provide food for him. "After all," he would muse to himself, "she's in the food business, isn't she?"

We all know people who assume someone else will take care of the house. Perhaps we all would like an absolutely clean house, always kept pure and fresh for us. But that's not how couples share responsibilities. Helping to keep up the house, whether outside maintenance, inside care or little chores such as putting dishes in the sink, picking up dirty laundry or putting towels where they belong comes with the territory. Wise marriage partners pick up after themselves, work hard and keep their house in order.

Marie and Don discussed their problem with a counselor. Marie is irritated and frustrated by Don's "peeled shrimp" attitude—"Someone else will take care of me; I won't have to worry about money, food, a clean house or an interrupted schedule." More enraging was his attitude of, "Don't bother me; I'm doing my own thing."

Marie's retort in their argument, "You'll have to peel your own shrimp," captures her frustration with the essence of the popular myth that "I'll do what I want to do, and the rest of the world can swirl around me." The trouble is that opportunities are missed while we protect our "right" to do as we please.

Not long ago I remember meeting with a couple who have a preschool age son. Both father and mother work, he for the city government, with a 7:00 a.m. to 3:00 p.m. schedule. The wife is a secretary in a retail computer store. They had protected the sanctity of their undisturbed schedules through the magic of video tape. The video recorder would tape two hours of her favorite afternoon television soaps. The schedule allowed their preschool age son to come home from day care with his father. Between 4:30 and 6:00 the son enjoyed either pre-recorded or video rented cartoons. An undisturbed network news show was the husband's occupation between 6:00 and 7:30. At 7:30, on came the recordings of the wife's afternoon soap operas. Everyone had a protected television schedule, and all seemed perfectly in order. The only problem was that all three family members were angry and irritable with each other. And they couldn't figure out why, as Christians, they didn't have quality family time.

A quick examination of how they spend time at home reveals they are poor stewards of their time and relationships by guarding their own video schedules. They expect their relationships to be somehow miraculously "taken care of" while they cling to their time-eating television habits.

Looking into Heaven

An unwillingness to peel your own shrimp is also manifested in preoccupation with the way things used to be or what might be. We all recall occasions when a good thing comes to an end. Like Jesus' ascension in Acts 1, we stand staring wistfully after the perfect vacation, the perfect sex experience or the child's first day at school. There is more to come, but we do not want to let go of the present moment. It is easier to stand looking into heaven than to get on with our tasks. We cling to the fading goodness because we know that when it is gone we will have to begin to peel our own shrimp. There are four aspects of married life that often catch us looking into the heavens when we should be looking down the road.

1. Nostalgia

Barbara kept a variety of pictures, some now faded, from her high school cheerleading days when she was young, trim and energetic. In the years since her graduation she continued to put on weight. Now she is clearly overweight. She keeps adding pounds as she "gazes into the heavens" of her high school cheerleading pictures.

All couples have real life changes, sometimes rather dramatic. The dreams of childhood, if we're not careful, become the nostalgic center of our lives. When we are off-center, focused on the past, we are oblivious to the opportunities God gives us. Many a retired athlete, whether amateur or professional, can quickly shed an unnoticed tear in remembering the glory days of the past. But life does go on, and and angel reminded the apostles at the time of Jesus' ascension not to look nostalgically into heaven at the rapidly vanishing, wonderful times with Jesus. They needed to be vigilant for Pentecost.

2. Self-Pity

For Kathy life seemed to end the day her husband, Richard, a young, healthy factory worker, was suddenly afflicted with a blood clot. Within 48 hours he was dead, leaving her and two young children to fend for themselves. Kathy and Richard had been raised in the church, both were Christians and considered theirs an ideal Christian family. But now, grief and remorse trapped Kathy. She was overwhelmed by the self-pity of, "How dare Richard abandon me and ruin the lives of my children!" She thought she would never be able to explain Richard's senseless death to two toddlers. Beyond photographs, they would never know their father. Kathy thought she deserved more than this from life. The two children needed a father to love, to romp with, to be a leader for them.

Self-pity is another form of refusing to peel your own shrimp. Unfortunately, from a human point-of-view, nobody owes us anything: money, health, family or a secure future. One can hope that in Kathy's church there will be some sensitive, loving, caring individuals who will help her move beyond the self-pity of looking into heaven wishing Richard were still here.

3. Refuse to Get on with Faithful Living

Don has childhood memories of his mother faithfully slaving over the kitchen stove and sink, preparing the shrimp of life so his father would always feel comfortable and taken care of. But those were different times. Don's mother was at home one hundred percent of the time. There was simply a different dynamic between Don's parents than what's expected of him and Marie.

Faithful living for Don first means understanding that his marriage is not going to duplicate his childhood home. Second, Don and Marie enjoy a more financially secure lifestyle. They take vacations, including a trip to the Holy Land, that their parents never enjoyed. But there is a price to be paid. There are no free lunches, no pre-peeled shrimp. If Don wants the simple lifestyle that his parents had, he either must give up the planned vacations or take more initiative to make them possible.

Fidelity to his marriage is more than not committing adultery. It's a matter of learning to peel the shrimp in his own household so that he and Marie can share the burdens of the day and make the marriage successful. Don needs to become more faithful to the realities of his and Marie's situation.

4. Can't Accept the Future

Another reason people stand spiritually and psychologically staring into the emptiness of past events is fear of the future. I recall visiting with one family who had lost a son in Vietnam. Suddenly three generations of family, including a grandparent and a younger sister, became over-possessive of the remaining son. They were afraid for Ted and afraid of being abandoned by God.

Ted was the youngest of four children and still in elementary school when his eighteen-year-old brother was killed. The trauma of Steve's death so enslaved the family that they simply would not allow Ted to grow up. During his teenage years Ted could do anything he wanted. There were cars, trips, clothes and concerts, and when school behavior problems were legion, Mom and Dad looked the other way. During his adolescent years it was wonderful, because his family peeled his shrimp for him.

Ted's first two marriages predictably ended in disaster. Now in an impassioned courtship with a woman he wants to marry, Ted and Stephanie are in serious trouble. If Ted marries, according to his mother, he may as well go to Vietnam. Neither she nor his father want to let go of him and will not allow any marriage to succeed, including their own, unless they learn to face family memories and move on.

Ted and his family can no longer protect themselves from either the past or the future. They have been swallowed up in the popular myth that "someone else will take care of me." Since God and the government didn't protect Steve from the aggressor's bullets, Ted and his family made an alliance to take care of each other, never to be hurt or vulnerable. Ted has been taken care of too well. The truth is, he's never learned to peel his own spiritual or emotional shrimp.

Insecurity

Sometimes marriage partners suffer from insecurity, feeling inadequate, unprepared, nervous and uncertain whether there is anything at all good in life and marriage.

Mary Ann and Dwight have been married for about six years. She is a country girl and he, a city boy. They met and married following an extended correspondence and courtship initiated at church camp, where they were both summer counselors. At a science fair in high school, Dwight decided that computers were the wave of the future and that he would take that career direction. Mary Ann is her father's girl. She knows how to run farm equipment and can repair almost anything from a field cultivator to broken china. An excellent cook, gardener and a nurturing individual, she and Dwight fell madly in love. The future seemed secure for both. But the computer business typically flourishes in the big city, not in the farm stable. Her alienation was not immediately evident in the relationship, but in retrospect Mary Ann says she felt like a fish out of water living in "Computer City" with Dwight. Her skills, likes and personal securities seemed to have abandoned her. The longer they lived in the city the less secure she was with her own skills.

Like the little boy who provided his lunch so Jesus could feed the five thousand, Mary Ann clearly had the two loaves and five fishes to feed multitudes of people in the church she attended in "Computer City." She had lived in a very secure environment in her small town setting. Her friends, children and family in her home town all dearly love her. Moving out of that environment made the daily tasks overwhelming. Dwight's energetic involvement in the city lifestyle increased her insecurity. She had begun to doubt her own capacity to prepare good meals, to be a good mother, a nurturing wife and an acceptable human being. She deeply loved Dwight and was anxious about their future.

In my discussions with the couple, we began to frame a plan whereby Mary Ann could acknowledge what everybody else knew—she could give something to others. We started with small, simple acts, such as preparing her favorite dish for church suppers. This was designed to counter the insecurity formed out of her naive myth that someone else, especially her family, always provide a secure environment.

Into every life come rain clouds, crises and even an occasional task of feeding five thousand when you feel unprepared, inadequate and helpless. Dale and his second wife, Connie, were at odds and couldn't solve their problems, so they called on their pastor for help. The source of the difficulty was quickly focused on Gretchen, Dale's nineteen-year-old daughter. The girl's mother had suffered a long illness that consumed tremendous amounts of family money and energy. Dale became very closely bonded with Gretchen during the crisis, and he would do everything within his power to make sure nothing would happen to her. He had not neglected his wife's health or welfare, but the grief and accumulated guilt over his first wife's painful demise and death made him overly sensitive to eliminating any crisis situations for Gretchen.

As a teenager, Gretchen was able to run wild because she was not being given good, disciplined examples. Some of her rebellion probably grew from her own fears that she would suffer the same fate as her mother. Dale, having lost one woman in his life, was fearful of losing Gretchen, both as a daughter and as an adult woman when she married.

Dale remarried when he spotted Connie. She is a successful, well-disciplined, healthy, energetic business executive. He believed she would take care of him and Gretchen. Dale needs to learn to face his life with the two women more directly. He has enough loaves and fishes to care for the family. But he needs to dispel the popular myth that his new wife will take care of him and provide instant security for Gretchen. Connie needs Dale to show her that he is fully capable of loving and giving to them.

Bringing Your Talents

Another of Jesus' parables is about the master who went to a far country, leaving one servant with one talent (a unit of currency), another with two and another with five (Matthew 25:14-30).

The two wise servants invested their talents and doubled their value. Upon the master's return one could show four talents, the other ten talents. The one-talent servant became caught in the inertia of his one talent. Fearful of losing it, he hurried to bury his talent. He was rejected for his overly conservative self-evaluation, ignoring his God-given talent and his own ability to peel his own shrimp and take care of himself. Inertia is a curse that makes our resources seem like less than we have. We are called to a life of activity. Neither the talent nor the master automatically took care of the servant.

So it is with marriages. Often the kind of talents we have and are valued for, we play too conservatively. We end up with less love, satisfaction and nurture than when we began. We have to offer our talents to the Lord if they are going to be blessed. Burying them is not going to help our families.

In sum, there are a variety of ways in which we become captured by the popular myth that someone else will take care of us. It may be Don's presumptive naivete that there would always be money, food, a clean house, an undisturbed schedule and someone to take care of him. Or we may become entrapped in the same myth through passively focusing on the past without looking to the future, where we could be blessed by marriage partners, families and God.

Finally, the third aspect of the myth is being trapped in our own insecurities so we doubt our abilities and talents. Through insecurity, ignored opportunities or inertia we become afraid to believe that what we hold in our lives and in our marriages is more than dirt and sand. In subtle ways we want someone else to transform our lives into something we're not.

Christian Truth:
Pick Up Your Bed and Walk

There are no easy marriages. People who brag about having lived for thirty years with a spouse without fighting are God's very special people, or they don't remember fights, or they are not telling the truth. Marriages may be made in heaven, but they are worked out on earth. The self-help literature on how to be successful in marriage, finances and health is more often a mirage than a miracle. We want to believe all the success testimonies, but by comparison we often feel we have failed.

Receive a Miracle

The proper thing to do is to put yourself in a place to receive a miracle. The people who received miracle healings from Jesus were those who, either by themselves or by the intercessory activity of their friends, were in a place where Jesus could bless them. The first step in receiving a miracle that empowers you to "pick up your bed and walk" begins by being in the right place at the right time.

The second step in receiving a miracle occurs when one partner reaches out and touches the other. Marie could have chosen to withdraw from Don and to stay angry at him, at God and at herself for trusting her husband to take care of himself. Instead of being consumed by her own disappointment, Marie has decided to reach out and work with Don to make the marriage successful. She's exhibiting the same kind of spiritually healthy initiative we see in the Syrophoenician woman who asked Jesus to cast the demon out of her daughter (Mark 7:24-30). Not easily put off, she understood the realities that the gospel had to be offered to the Jews before the Gentiles. But she also understood, even as Marie understands her relationship with Don, that those who appear to be least deserving may receive "the crumbs under the table."

Marie could resort to being self-righteous and vindictive toward Don, denying him shrimp, bread crumbs or herself. However, she loves her husband and so once again will minister to him for the sake of the marriage and for the sake of the kingdom of God. Marie's prayer would be that her husband Don would put himself in a place to receive the full blessing of his faith. The measure of that would be his willingness to pick up his bed and walk.

In Matthew 7:7 Jesus, in the Sermon on the Mount, admonishes his believers to ask for things of the kingdom, and they will be given to them. In Don's case the issue is not whether either God or Marie will always provide him with peeled shrimp. What Don wants most is to be loved and respected by his wife. He must learn that there are more appropriate ways of receiving that love than swiping pre-peeled shrimp from the refrigerator.

Don needs to ask of himself first what might he do to bless Marie, and thereby receive the greater gift from her. Putting yourself in a place to receive a miracle in marriage means you must be willing to show some good faith toward your marriage partner. Marie does not want Don to be a housemaid; however, she would appreciate consideration and affirmation.

"Ask and it shall be given unto you" is the biblical principle that tells us to be active in receiving a blessing. We must be neither passive nor grasping.

Some Christians are too passive spiritually. They sit like bumps on a log waiting like Don, or the unwise virgins, for someone else always to peel their shrimp for them or bring the wedding feast to them. Others are so aggressive they become like the impulsive Peter, grasping at spiritual or marital straws. One doesn't grasp the kingdom by jerking out of joints; we need to ask and receive gladly.

It is a far cry from works righteousness to ask, to knock and to step forward to receive. We recall the account when Jesus healed the ten lepers. One would think that all of them would be eternally grateful. But only one of the ten actually picked up his spiritual bed and walked by coming back to thank Jesus, fully receiving the blessing of the healing. Asking for a spiritual or marital miracle is not simply taking. It is actively putting yourself in a place to receive the blessings of life with grace and gratitude.

Many of the wedlock deadlocks begin to thaw out and then freeze up again. The secret to breaking the marital gridlock of giving and receiving is that, having received, move immediately to give. That sets up a chain reaction in which both parties begin to experience the reality "it is more blessed to give than to receive."

Curtailing Activities

In the case of Sarah and Kyle, Kyle realized he needed to give his wife some of the tender loving care he so spontaneously shared with his office colleagues, his civic group and the little league softball team he was coaching. Having received the insight, blessing and forgiveness of his wife for his inadvertent exclusion of her, Kyle picked up his bed and began to return his blessing by resigning his position as coach of the little league softball team and curtailing the long hours of involvement in civic organizations. He made certain that his boy scout good deeds for office colleagues were limited. By doing this, Kyle was able to give to Sarah a blessing that made her feel secure. The positive dynamic of "having received . . . give" began to correct the marriage and to send it off in a positive direction.

Not all are called to be pioneers in business, a profession or the arts. Some of us are called to provide supportive activities. Our tasks may not be as glamorous as going out to slay the dragons of the world. Our spouses, instead, may be in a position to advance their careers and need to be nurtured, fed and supported.

In the case of Brian and Beverly, he has made a self-conscious decision to support his wife's career. And that means supporting her need to be on the road and attend seminars. She, not Brian of course, gathers the annual bonuses and the accolades at the company sponsored week-long vacation in the Bahamas for the best performers. If Brian is not careful he could easily become resentful, because he is not on the front lines of the career-enhancing activities.

Brian and Beverly must work out an agreement by which he becomes active in cultural, athletic, church and civic activities in his hometown so that he too is nurtured. When his wife is in town he will have something to give to her beyond encouragement and taking care of their son.

Brian needs to receive in order to give. In some ways his needs for receiving will require more energy because the accolades and salary increments in his job simply will not even parallel those of his wife. His role in this marriage, in terms of outward appearance, will be strictly a supporting cast role. If he and Beverly do not make certain they have time together when she comes home, neither will have the experience of receiving, and both will find it difficult to give to the other.

In such cases I highly recommend that when one marriage partner has been out of town for an extended period of time, a couple should secure a baby-sitter. The spouses should meet at their earliest convenience after the airplane touches down or the car rolls into the driveway and spend at least two hours together at a restaurant or a ball game, doing something together so that they get reacquainted before the various administrative tasks of running a household intrude. Where one family member is highly dependent on the other marriage partner, it is important that each learns to peel his or her own shrimp, not to devour it selfishly, but to give to one another. Therein lies the blessing of passing the shrimp and the peace.

The goal of the good marriage is to increase and multiply the benefits and graces for all. Taking initiative to offer the talents, gifts and love that you have for the marriage partner is a way of picking up your bed and walking. The scenario of falsely believing that someone will/must take care of you becomes broken. Unselfish giving breaks that deadlock, and blessings will flow.

Responsible for Your Behavior

Taking care of yourself, peeling your own shrimp, is not an

admonition to selfishness. This is a declaration that one must learn to be responsible for one's own behavior. I remember counseling one couple in which the wife was constantly nagging her husband, Dennis, about his messy auto mechanic's repair shop. At least two to five times a week Loretta would visit him at work and offer perceptive but demanding suggestions about how his supplies might be more neatly stocked and his counter more cleanly arranged. The idea of nuts, bolts, pieces of sheet metal and the innards of engines lying all around the work area floor did not fail to escape her attention. She commented regularly about how he could be more efficient, make more money and be a better husband if he would run his business like she wanted him to. He would nod and follow some of the suggestions, but his work place was never as neat as his wife wanted. Dennis seemed unruffled by Loretta's badgering. But, by his own admission, he did not feel close to her. She was involved in raising the children, perhaps over-committed to a variety of church activities and certainly enjoying her free time at home.

The light dawned on me one day when Loretta was out of town for a week with their teenage daughter. Dennis was talking to me about a new addition he was putting on the house as a surprise for Loretta. He assembled all of his construction buddies in hopes of getting the new room built and ready to go up in the week that she was gone. At one point he shrugged his shoulders and said, "I don't know whether this will really help Loretta feel better about herself or make any difference anyway." I pushed the comment and discovered—almost to my disbelief—that Dennis' portion of the bedroom was kept relatively clean. Loretta's closet, her bathroom, the sewing room and the kitchen, however, were in a steady state of chaos. Clothes were scattered, unclean dishes were piled up and a general clutter prevailed.

If Loretta is concerned about improving her relationship with Dennis, she's going to have to learn the responsibility of cleaning up after herself. She has become a victim of seeing the splinter in her husband's eye but failing to recognize the log in her own. If she doesn't learn to take care of herself, she's in an excellent position to become a marital martyr. And if her projection is not corrected, eventually she will complain that she wants out of the marriage because Dennis is not taking care of himself. Perhaps at a subtle level she hopes that if her husband's garage can be neat and orderly, he will have the time and energy to take care of her home responsibilities so that her space will be clean too. But Loretta needs to reverse her thinking and take care of her responsibilities.

One blessing that comes to a couple finally able to be responsible for themselves is the experience of an abundant life. The little boy who came to hear Jesus preach brought Jesus his lunch, not a convoy of refrigerated trucks filled with Marshall Plan relief supplies. The abundant life for this lad came because he had planned for that day—he was taking care of himself by bringing fish and loaves, and he was willing to share. The devastating effects of always being in debt financially, spiritually and emotionally diminish the possibility of abundant life. A simple swing of the pendulum eliminates worrying about feeding the whole crowd and empowers one to enjoy today's lunch. God will bless a marriage and nourish it with new life.

Having peeled his own shrimp before leaving home, the young boy not only was able to give what Jesus needed in the moment, but many hundreds of blessings were also poured out. And "many full baskets were left over." Such is the case in the marriage relationship.

In the case of Marsha and Jeff, one of their unpeeled shrimp was their attitude toward their daughter. Both loved her, but for a long time each was so wrapped up in their private concerns and commitments outside the family that the daughter was neglected. And Paula, the daughter, was both hurt and resentful.

However, Marsha and Jeff began to discover that when they could affirm each other, what psychologists call a "reciprocal transformation" took place. The good things fed off each other. Marsha and Jeff were transformed because they were not so demanding of each other. In turn their transformed relationship became a real blessing for Paula. In the miracle story of the feeding of the five thousand, the food far exceeded the most immediate need and expectation. So it is with marriage relationships. If either husband or wife is willing to take up the bed and walk, the immediate needs are cared for abundantly and other needs are fulfilled.

Life is not a catered event for either husband or wife. As wrong as it is for Don to sit home in front of the television gorging himself on Marie's shrimp, it is no less a sin for Loretta to have her house strung with used clothes, dishes and unfinished projects waiting there for Dennis to come home and clean up. If both Loretta and Don will begin to take responsibility for themselves, the dramatic, positive effects on their spouses, Dennis and Marie, will be immediately evidenced. That's the point of the miracle story for developing strong marriages.

In Sum

Many Christians can and have married well. The fallacy comes in believing that having chosen well or been chosen well by a mate, life will take care of itself. But getting married is only the beginning. The initial decision, the wedding ceremony and the honeymoon only succeed in getting the characters on stage. The drama begins after that.

One needs to be actively responsible for oneself and radically and positively transform the beliefs, attitudes and self-esteem of the spouse. By only being on the receiving end, either spouse loses self, miracles and the blessings a Christian marriage can bring. It locks up the marriage and fails to break the deadlocks.

Taking the initiative to think of and act on behalf of another is immensely satisfying. The gridlocks and deadlocks occur when a partner, either through digging in his or her heels or falling into a pattern of unwise stewardship, enters into a pact of passivity in which the other partner has to do all the work of caring, loving, nurturing and thinking ahead for the partnership.

Breaking that wedlock deadlock calls for putting aside the popular myth that someone else will take care of you regardless of how well you are situated. We are called to adopt the Christian truth that, having been blessed by the miracle of a Christian marriage, we pick up our beds and walk. In so doing, both the marriage relationship and the marital partners receive blessings beyond their deepest expectations.

Conclusion

In this book on obtaining freedom from deadlocked marriages we have explored the myths that captivate and deceive us. Myths are always bigger than life, and when we become confused and anxious we will hide either behind moralistic myths or escapist myths because the truth is too much for us to handle directly.

The truth that frees us from the bondage of the popular secular and Christian myths comes from the truth we find first of all in God's encounter with human beings in the Old and New Testaments. The truths of the gospel are like mirrors that we must look into first to face God, then to face ourselves. Sometimes we see painful truths and sometimes we see ones that are releasing: We are more right than we thought.

One might reorganize these eight classic conflicts of Christian marriage into three major clusters to help you further identify and correctly work through them so your marriage may experience the freedom that is available to you.

The first major cluster relates to leadership, power and control. many Christian couples fight over how their family is to be run. When in trouble, either the husband or wife appeals to some Scripture reference or teaching to support the position argued. However, the question should not be who is going to win the spiritual argument. The real issue is the mutual discovery that men and women are frequently different in ways that go beyond sex and sexuality. Some women are simply more aggressive and assertive than their husbands. But this complementarity can be a real source of strength if the husband or the wife does not try to force the spousea to fit a pre-existing stereotype. The goal is to enhance mutual respect, not to see who wins.

In the second category, sex often becomes the escape or the scapegoat for struggles involving leadership, parenting, financial concerns, sense of failure or feelings of abandonment. Adultery or the compulsion to use sex to fulfill an agenda other than delightful, sensuous satisfaction can be a real pitfall in a marriage. When a couple concentrates on transforming sexual motives instead sexual technique, other conflicts will be put in proper perspective and sex will be the enjoyable experience it is intended to be.

A third major area of wedlock deadlock pertains to responsibility. It is easy to hid behind the children, making them the excuse or hiding behind the expertise of a clergyperson, marriage counselor or attorney. These appeals to toher authorities, including parental obligations, is an evasion of one's responsibility in the marriage. The passive dependent and manipulative behavior symbolized by expecting someone else to "peel the shrimp of life" also characterizes an evasion or responsibility. In this area of life, shouldering the responsibility to be both mature and sensitive in our marriage relationships gives us freedom from deadlock.

In each of these major areas, we have ready-made theological and scriptural excuses to defend our inadequate and immature behavior. I hope this book—its organization and the themes presented—will become a source of liberation for Christian marriages so life and faith may be lived to the fullest.